DATE DUE

THE FOUR PILLARS OF

PROFIT-DRIVEN MARKETING

HOW TO MAXIMIZE CREATIVITY, ACCOUNTABILITY, AND ROI

LESLIE H. MOELLER AND **EDWARD C. LANDRY**
PARTNERS, BOOZ & COMPANY
with **THEODORE KINNI**

New York   Chicago   San Francisco   Lisbon   London   Madrid
Mexico City   Milan   New Delhi   San Juan   Seoul
Singapore   Sydney   Toronto

The *McGraw·Hill* Companies

Copyright © 2009 by Booz & Company. All rights reserved. Printed in the United States of America. Except as permitted under the United States Copyright Act of 1976, no part of this publication may be reproduced or distributed in any form or by any means, or stored in a data base or retrieval system, without the prior written permission of the publisher.

1 2 3 4 5 6 7 8 9 0   DOC/DOC   0 1 0 9 8

ISBN 978-0-07-161505-1
MHID 0-07-161505-9

McGraw-Hill books are available at special quantity discounts to use as premiums and sales promotions, or for use in corporate training programs. To contact a representative please visit the Contact Us pages at www.mhprofessional.com.

This book is printed on acid-free paper.

Library of Congress Cataloging-in-Publication Data

Moeller, Leslie H., 1961–
    The four pillars of profit-driven marketing: how to maximize creativity, accountability, and ROI / by Leslie H. Moeller & Edward C. Landry; with Theodore Kinni.
        p. cm.
    ISBN 0-07-161505-9 (alk. paper)
    1. Marketing—Management. 2. Communication in marketing. 3. Rate of return. 4. Profit. I. Landry, Edward C., 1965– II. Kinni, Theodore B., 1956– III. Title.
    HF5415 13.M59 2009
    658.8—dc22

                                                            2008031080

Booz & Company values the confidentiality of our clients. We do not share information about the organizations we serve. The specific examples of our client work cited in this book were used only with explicit permission generously granted by those companies.

Contents

CONTENTS

Acknowledgments

First, we must thank our publisher at McGraw-Hill, Herb Schaffner, who spotted the potential of this book, and editor Donya Dickerson, who has been an enthusiastic advocate and an able guide as we worked through the final revision of the manuscript. We would also like to acknowledge the efforts of Jim Levine, our agent and principal in the Levine Greenberg Literary Agency, who led us through the vagaries of the publishing world.

We owe much to the team at *strategy + business*, our quarterly magazine, including publisher Jon Gage, who ably managed every aspect of the business of this business book, saving us much time and many headaches in the process, and marketing manager Alan Shapiro who will help us bring the book to the attention of the world at large. Art Kleiner, editor-in-chief of *strategy + business*, read the manuscript as many times as we did and each time raised its quality with elegant edits and perceptive comments.

We thank *s + b* alumnus Randall Rothenberg, now the CEO of the Interactive Advertising Bureau, who conceived the article that was the seed for this book and nourished the book through its infancy, as well as Thom Forbes, who conducted much of the original research and interviews and helped write early chapter drafts.

The logistics of writing a business book are surprisingly complex, so we were very lucky to have Lisa Mitchell, the director of the firm's Marketing & Sales Service Offering, on our team. Lisa kept us and the many strands of this project, from schedules to graphics to permissions, in order. Her ideas and comments added just as much value to the contents of the book.

We send many thanks to our partners at Booz & Company for sharing an institution committed to excellence in everything we do and informing our thinking on so many levels. Thanks also to Nikhil Bahadur, Steve Treppo, and all our team members in the Consumer & Media practice for refining and improving our ideas and doing whatever it took to deliver results. Special thanks go to Gregor Harter and Andrew Tipping, who along with Ed, developed *CMO Thought Leaders*, the *s + b* Reader from which we borrowed relevant insights and many of the CMO quotes found in this book.

A debt of gratitude is owed to our many clients whose experiences and successes informed the perspective that now is *The Four Pillars of Profit-Driven Marketing*. We are particularly indebted to: current and former Kellogg managers and executives, including Scott Barnes, Brad Bjorndahl, Jim Burt, Dan Doore, Bob Dow, Pete Galster, Mike Greene, Carolyn Gawlinski Hendricksma, Sue Karibjanian, Tom Knowlton, Dale Lazarro, Amjad Malik, Kevin Reeser, Phil Straniero, and Adonis Vergara; Harrah's CEO and chairman Gary Loveman and former SVP of New Business Development Richard Mirman; John Porter; and

Dudley Ruch. Their generosity in sharing their time and allowing us to write about their companies and experiences made this a better book.

Finally, as with our every endeavor, our families deserve special recognition for their support throughout the entire process of writing and publishing this book. Les sends his love and gratitude to Jennifer, Abigail, Hunter, and Stefen for sharing him with a job so time intensive that writing a book was just another drop in the bucket. Ed wants to express his appreciation to his four children, Erica, Julia, Scott, and Alex, who provide inspiration for everything he does, and to Anita Landry, his wife, who provides both invaluable family support and sharp insights that have found their way into this book and also into several articles published over the last years.

Marketing's Fifth "P"

A half-century ago, a young marketing professor named E. Jerome McCarthy neatly poured the variables of the marketing mix into four buckets: product, price, place, and promotion. Today, in Marketing 101, aspiring marketers still learn McCarthy's Four Ps. Their job, they are taught, is to manipulate these four variables to create and deliver offers that customers find compelling. That's all well and good, but there is also a fifth, most critical "P" that isn't explicitly described. This is the "P" that enables a business to grow, that moves share price and, ultimately, ensures corporate survival. It's *profit*.

Typically in Marketing 101, profit is taken for granted. The buried assumption is that if you optimize your marketing mix, you will connect with customers, sell more of whatever it is you sell, and thus, earn more profit. In the real world, however, it is entirely possible—common, in fact—for marketers to invest in perfecting their products, setting an irresistible price, expanding their distribution channels, or blitzing the airwaves with advertising and not earn back their costs, let alone a profit. Their marketing does not produce the results that they anticipated and paid for, and far too often they either don't know it or they don't know why until it is too late to fix it.

Take the major clothing retailer that Wharton accounting professors David Larcker and Christopher Ittner studied in

2004. Larcker and Ittner analyzed the retailer's returns on its investments in TV, radio, and print advertising. They found that the company's TV ads outperformed radio and print in terms of return on investment (ROI). Unfortunately, they also discovered that *none* of the three advertising vehicles generated a positive ROI. A dollar spent on advertising generated less than a dollar in sales no matter what the media platform.

Or consider Blockbuster, whose entire business model has come under extreme pressure as its customers are offered increasingly convenient ways to obtain the movies and games it rents. To combat this, on January 1, 2005, the company announced its "No late fees" marketing initiative. It spent $50 million promoting the program, which it estimated would cost it another $250 million to $300 million in lost late fees, but which management believed would deliver a positive ROI by driving rental volume and retail sales. The actual result: annual revenues in 2005 decreased 3.1 percent compared to 2004; Blockbuster's share price, which opened at $9.35 in January 3, 2005, ended the year at $3.75.

In yet another case: in the late 1990s, in its quest to maintain its market share, Kellogg Company analyzed a year's worth of trade promotions—the deals made with retailers to get products prominently displayed, promoted, discounted, and featured in local advertising and circulars. It discovered that 59 percent of its trade promotion events lost money. The only bright spot was that the losers didn't gobble up all of the returns generated by the remaining 41 percent.[1] (Kellogg, as you will see in Chapter 8, resolved that problem.)

These aren't isolated incidents. Kellogg's marketing results, for example, were actually better than those of many of its competitors. Based on our experience and analyses done by companies themselves, we estimate that trade spending by major consumer packaged goods manufacturers has an average short-term ROI of *negative* 20 percent—that is, for every dollar they spend to generate volume, their return is 80 cents. The Big Three automobile manufacturers have a similar problem. Even before the current meltdown, they had more than tripled the incentives they offered customers since 1990, to nearly $3,800 per vehicle, or 14 percent of the average sales price, according to CNW Marketing Research. Yet Detroit continued to lose share in the United States (by 1.6 percentage points in 2002 alone, prior to the recent precipitous rise in oil prices) to imports whose incentives were half as high.

The nebulous and too-often-negative return on marketing spend isn't a new problem, but it has been significantly exacerbated over the last several years, in particular, by the fragmentation of media. Today's marketers must cope with many more variables in their investment decision processes than their predecessors did. Think of all the newly emerging and largely unproven vehicles represented by Web- and e-mail–based venues alone. How much of your marketing spend should be allocated to search, to e-mail campaigns, to blogs, to mobile? How does advertising in popular digital "worlds," such as MTV's Nicktropolis, Virtual Lower East Side, and Second Life translate into consideration or trial or any of the traditional steps in creating a loyal customer in the real world? And how does this so-called new media fit into the traditional marketing mix of TV, radio, and print?

And look at the stakes. Estimates of the total annual marketing spend of U.S. companies range from $600 billion to over $1 trillion. *Advertising Age* calculated that the 10 leading national advertisers spent over $29 billion in the United States alone in 2007. Advertising and media, trade promotion, and consumer promotion spending routinely account for as much as 20 percent to 40 percent of sales among consumer packaged goods (CPG) companies in the United States, up from 15 percent in 1978. The spending against all Four Ps can be the largest expense on the profit and loss statement for most of these companies, and certainly it is in the top two, depending on the size of cost of goods sold.

"It's all about growth," says Rob Malcolm, president of global marketing, sales, and innovation for Diageo, the world's leading premium drinks business. "But not growth at all costs. It's all about profitable growth that delivers returns to shareholders." That, in a nutshell, is the aim of *The Four Pillars of Profit-Driven Marketing*.

This book is about the application of marketing ROI—a combination of modern measurement technologies and contemporary organizational design that enables companies to understand, quantify, and optimize their marketing spending and thus forge better connections with customers. It integrates analytic firepower, decision support, processes, and people development together in a quest for improved returns. These improved returns are achieved by better directing resources toward the marketing executions, pricing, product adaptations, vehicles, and/or geographies that will generate sales most profitably.

Unlike the intuitive decision making on which marketers have depended in the past, marketing ROI is not a hypothesis about consumer response. It is the most tangible and meaningful measure of response—whether people will part with cash for your product or service. For this reason, ROI actually has the power to tell marketers what consumers will pay for something, as well as informing and funding the creative efforts needed to gain their attention. But this is not a new idea in and of itself;

quantifying the return on spending has been the Holy Grail of marketing for some time. What is new and noteworthy about *The Four Pillars of Profit-Driven Marketing* is that it offers a proven implementation framework that can help marketers capture these essential metrics and utilize the insights they yield to better connect with customers and improve their creativity, accountability, and ROI.

This task is not easy. In fact, given the magnitude and the stakes of the ROI challenge in marketing, it is entirely understandable that some marketers have tried to cope by sidestepping it altogether or obscuring it with smoke and mirrors. "Marketing is intuitive," they say in order to justify throwing dollars into the mix in a random effort to find something, anything, that works. When asked about the ROI of their efforts, they say, "Marketing is not a science, it's an art. There's no way to measure the results." And, if and when unacceptable ROI levels are exposed, they say, "It's not about the short term. We're building brand awareness." If you are a marketing executive who is frustrated with having to fall back on excuses like these, or a CEO, CFO, or board member who is tired of hearing them, this book was written for you.

There is, by the way, no need to disguise this book in a brown paper wrapper. If you are concerned with measuring the return on your marketing investments and optimizing the allocation of your spend, you are not alone. Ongoing studies by Booz & Company and the Association of National Advertisers (ANA) reveal that 90 percent of marketing and nonmarketing executives across nine industries believe that marketing is challenged to measure effectiveness; 81 percent say that the pressure to measure effectiveness has increased to a moderate or large extent over the past three years.

Much of the pressure to increase marketing's effectiveness is coming from marketers themselves. Jim Stengel, the former chief marketing officer of Procter & Gamble (P&G), will tell you that the development of the capability that enables marketing accountability is one of the top priorities of P&G as an organization. And remember, this is coming from a leading CPG company whose marketing prowess has already driven decades of high performance and which has produced many of the discipline's most accomplished practitioners. Stengel, in his capacity as chairman of the ANA's board of directors, was instrumental in the formation of its Marketing Accountability Task Force and hosted its members, drawn from 20 leading companies in diverse industries, at P&G headquarters in Cincinnati. Here's the pithy first finding of the task force's 2005 study:

> Every other function is held accountable for its return on investment. No longer can marketing expect a free pass from management and shareholders. Marketing is competing with every other function within the company for a limited pool of shareholder dollars. If this function alone cannot or will not prove its relative efficiency, management will not keep feeding the beast.[2]

That's a theme that we are hearing over and over from marketers. The first of the top 10 challenges facing marketers, according to a Chief Marketing Officer (CMO) Council's survey, *Marketing Outlook 2007*, is "quantify and measure the value of marketing programs and investments."[3]

Clearly, the pressure to increase marketing effectiveness is also coming from CEOs. Philip Kotler, the S.C. Johnson & Son Professor of International Marketing at Northwestern University's Kellogg School of Management, echoed the findings of the ANA task force when he wrote, "CEOs are understandably growing impatient with marketing. They feel that they get accountability for their investments in finance, production, information technology, even purchasing, but don't know what their marketing spending is achieving."[4]

Boards of directors are running out of patience, too, as evidenced by the short tenure of many CEOs and the even shorter tenure of many CMOs (as we will see in Chapter 1). When the CMO Council surveyed board members in 2007, they pointed to these four reasons why CMOs fail in the current environment: no real authority or clout; lack of credibility and respect; inability to work with the CEO; and the lack of "value-added perspectives."[5] Further, many observers believe that boards are starting to take a harder look at the role and impact of the CMO in the companies over which they preside. For instance, Harvard Business School professors John Quelch and Gail McGovern, who sit on six corporate boards themselves, are convinced that board attention on marketing is bound to become more focused and intense. They write: "Boards must measure the health of their corporate brands, the health of their companies' customer relationships, and the effectiveness of their marketing expenditures."[6]

In short, the current state of marketing is exactly what you would expect from a function in which ROI has been ignored for too long: suboptimal and often unknown returns, increasing complexity, higher financial stakes, intensifying performance pressure, and too little actual knowledge of customer preferences put to use in product launches and campaigns. This is the working environment of today's marketers. It is also the landscape that we intend to help you escape through the system presented in this book.

There are a few companies that have already staked highly profitable claims in the rapidly expanding territory of marketing

ROI. Some, particularly CPG companies, which have traditionally depended on their marketing functions to differentiate their products and drive growth, have been pursuing better customer connections through marketing ROI for several decades. Marketers at these companies have added measurement to their traditional tasks of gaining customer insight and generating creative responses. Other companies have focused on ROI and accountability more recently, but are literally inventing and reinventing themselves as a result of the breadth and intensity of their efforts. A well-known example, discussed in Chapter 3, is Capital One Financial Corporation, a Fortune 500 company that is justly famous for the successful use of marketing analytics. Among the other cases we will explore are Harrah's Entertainment, Kellogg Company, and Korea's LG Electronics.

These companies are operating in diverse businesses and geographies, but one thing that they all are seeking is a robust understanding of marketing ROI. They realize that ROI analytics are not black boxes that, once purchased, magically and without any effort or change on their parts produce profitability. They know that ROI is more than a number, that it also represents a mindset and an organizational capability, which, in addition to sophisticated analytics, requires decision support tools, processes, and organizational support and alignment to produce the insights that lead to profitable customer relationships.

Marketers who mistake ROI for anything less than a capability artificially limit their own results. Yes, they can still measure the success of their marketing events. But, they cannot make the all-important connection between the measurement of success and the continuous improvement of marketing profitability. It is the fully developed and aligned capability that transforms the marketing process of insight, creation, communication, and measurement into a closed loop and virtuous cycle. In this more robust view of marketing, ROI also represents learning and knowledge. Its application enables marketers to determine which responses work best and to apply that knowledge to the process of refining insights and improving future responses, as well as rationalizing the allocation of their spending and optimizing their returns.

Marketing ROI as a corporate capability is a concept that continues to emerge and evolve as we write these words. As we'll see, its theoretical roots stretch back centuries, but the technology that allows marketers to put theory into practice is considerably newer. Computing power; rich, consistent streams of data; and analytic and decision support software have made the application of marketing ROI to performance improvement an achievable reality in the past 20 or so years. In fact, Booz & Company, in its work with clients, built pioneering applications designed to help measure and apply the ROI of marketing, pricing, and promotion spending. These tools, which are capable of complex modeling jobs such as analyzing the entire marketing mix, continue to evolve, becoming more powerful as well as easier and more intuitive to use.

In the coming years, many other companies will join the rather sparse ranks of today's ROI marketers as they seek to create and optimize their bonds with customers and increase their return on marketing investments. Now is a good time to start this journey. For one thing, the value of marketing ROI is proven: it helped a leading pharmaceutical company produce a nearly 5 percent increase in operating profitability over a one-year period by reallocating resources for medical education, detailing, and patient support services across physician and patient segments; a Fortune 500 food products company earn sustained benefits of

$65 million to $70 million over a three-year period and boost volume by over 7 percent in accounts that undertook analytic planning; and an industry-leading brewer to save 20 percent by better understanding the cost/benefit trade-offs over five marketing vehicles.

For another thing, the capabilities needed to implement and utilize ROI marketing are not yet commonplace. As we will see in greater detail in Chapter 1, the majority of marketers—68 percent, according to a survey by the CMO Council—are unable to determine the profitability of an event, the indivisible unit of marketing ROI analysis such an online banner ad on a specific Web site or a single billboard or a sampling promotion in a specific store. In fact, 30 to 50 percent of the marketing executives we meet can't place an accurate figure on the aggregate advertising and promotion for their business.

Of course, sophisticated business analytics, including marketing ROI, are complex, continuously evolving, and often difficult to implement—a reality that companies that succeed with them can turn to their advantage. When Tom Davenport, the President's Distinguished Professor of Information Technology and Management at Babson College, searched out companies "that were successful both in terms of their overall performance and in their use of business analytics," he focused on 32 companies that fit the bill. Of those companies, only 11 qualified as what Davenport labels "analytical competitors" in marketing or any other strategic endeavor. In his 2007 book, *Competing on Analytics*, he defines an analytic competitor as "an organization that uses analytics extensively and systematically to outthink and outexecute the competition."[7] We think marketing is a logical place to start building such a corporatewide capability: it is often a greenfield in terms of implementation and the top- and bottom-line rewards are direct. Further, the event-based nature of marketing (a characteristic we will explain in greater detail in Chapter 2) makes it a fertile function for the kinds of experimentation and pilot programs that are needed to discover the value of a business analytics capability, as well as build support for it within the organizations.

While the ROI of marketing ROI is very attractive (companies often realize benefits ranging from 10 to 30 percent of their marketing spend), we wouldn't want to leave this introduction without reiterating the fact that building this capability is very hard work. It encompasses the exacting job of analyzing a brand and the products and services that comprise it; communicating its benefits to various, noncontiguous customer groups including distributors, retailers, and consumers; developing systems and processes to continually refresh these communications activities; measuring the results; and using measurements to continuously improve. It demands investments in specialized knowledge, data acquisition, and information technologies. It requires the integration of revamped processes supported by skills, training, and incentives. But, of course, if marketing that stimulates creativity, encourages accountability, and optimizes profitability was easy, it wouldn't be such a rewarding competitive advantage.

WHAT LIES AHEAD

Before we move forward, a brief overview of the coming chapters may be helpful.

Chapter 1 describes the pressures facing marketers: how the pressing need for organic growth and shifting tides of competitive advantage have made the marketing function more important than ever; how the changing demands of consumers, the demassification of mass media, and the need for both a long- and short-term perspective have made marketing more complex than ever; and how these pressures are impacting the organizational and career security of marketers. It will show how marketing ROI enables marketers to cope with these pressures.

Chapter 2 explores the functional context of marketing ROI and clears away the smoke and mirrors that obscure what you get for the money you spend. It deconstructs the marketing process and describes its four main tasks: insight, creation, communication, and measurement. Then, it shows how ROI is calculated and how it can enhance the marketer's performance of each of these tasks, further illustrating the essential role ROI plays in marketing microeconomics. Finally, it explores the primary reasons why more marketers have not developed this capability.

In Chapter 3, you will visit ROI marketers, such as Capital One, and learn about how they approach marketing. This chapter describes the mindset that evolves within companies that successfully develop this capacity. It also introduces the four pillars needed to develop and support the ROI capability: *analytics*; the *systems and tools* needed to deploy analytics; *processes* that define the analyses and ensure action in the proper sequence; and the *organizational alignment*, skills, and incentives needed to motivate the organization to execute the processes.

Chapters 4 through 7 are dedicated to exploring these four pillars in greater depth. Chapter 4 describes the development of the analytical power that ROI marketers are able to wield today. It demystifies the "black box" view of analytics as well as the barriers that marketers often trip over in their rush to obtain them. It offers a practical approach to classifying and understanding the three broad classes of analytics (behavioral, attitudinal, and business case) and the four types of data they require: event cost, profitability, transactional data, and attitudinal data. And it discusses how to choose between them based on your industry, data availability, and your internal capabilities.

Chapter 5 is devoted to the decision support tools that enable ROI marketers to put their analytic measures to work. These tools are the enabling systems that reduce complexity and make it easy to grasp and manipulate data. It describes the three principle types of decision support (DS) systems and tools: planning; execution; and post-event analysis. And it considers the primary issues in developing and choosing between DS tools, including whether and how to integrate them into your existing systems and the critical prerequisites for maximizing the accuracy of their results. Finally, because DS tools are evolving so rapidly, this chapter discusses trends in their development and the software capabilities that will be appearing in the near future.

Chapters 6 and 7 are devoted to the two pillars—processes and organizational alignment, respectively—that too many marketers ignore in their rush to capture the competitive advantages of marketing ROI analytics. The problem is that while analytics and DS tools are very powerful, until they are properly integrated into your company's marketing processes and those processes are rigorously executed, you cannot gain their full benefit. In fact, when the two final pillars are not fully considered and developed, the analytics and tools become marginalized and eventually ignored. Companies in which this happens have raw ROI competency, but it never evolves into a full-fledged capability. They obtain the knowledge, but find it difficult, if not impossible, to act upon it to create and enhance customer connections.

Chapter 6 is devoted to the processes that integrate analytics and tools into everyday marketing operations. Processes are the glue that holds the components of marketing ROI together.

This chapter describes how these processes differ from typical marketing processes. It also explores the objectives and requirements of each of the four processes (targeting setting, planning, execution, and post-event analysis) needed to capture ROI results and fully utilize the knowledge encompassed within them.

Chapter 7 describes the organizational elements that ensure that people collect and analyze data, use decision support tools, and execute processes. This final pillar addresses the ever-present conundrum of organizational acceptance and compliance. It explores key issues in organizational alignment and support of marketing ROI such as the concentric rings of success and support needed to develop ROI expertise across and beyond the marketing function, the development of a center of excellence that will house your analytical firepower, the various roles and responsibilities that people must assume to staff processes and ensure execution, and alignment of corporate policy, such as incentives, to support the creation of marketing that connects.

The subject of Chapter 8, the book's final chapter, is the transformative and developmental path that is required to begin building the full marketing ROI capacity. It describes a six-step process you can use to get your marketing ROI initiative off to a strong start and illustrates that process with a case study drawn from the Kellogg Company's work with trade promotions.

It is our intention to convince you that marketing ROI makes sense for you and your company and that it is worth the journey. We will also guide you through the beginnings of the journey and help you avoid the pitfalls that have tripped up those marketers who have gone before. By the time you reach the final pages of the book, it is our hope that you will have become a marketing ROI convert and champion.

Chapter 1

The Marketer's Challenge

The craft of marketing has not kept pace with the changing world in which marketers ply their trade. In fact, the disconnect between the environment and the craft has become so pronounced that the need to predict and measure results, impose order on and optimize marketing spending, and continuously improve customer insights and creative responses has become a matter of urgent concern.

The theory and practice of marketing management as a science first gelled in the 1950s. It was designed for an *Ozzie and Harriet* world where the nuclear family was still intact and happily migrating to new homes in the fast-expanding suburbs. Everybody read magazines such as *Life* or the *Saturday Evening Post*, subscribed to the local newspaper, and watched the Big Three television networks. The marketer's stock in trade was his or her ability to influence a monolithic, easy-to-reach market.

The 1960s celebrated iconoclasm, but, from the marketer's perspective, little had changed. Marketers had to learn the language of a new generation, but once they were fluent, they discovered that the baby boomers consumed goods with an appetite unmatched in history. A brand could still hitch its star to a clever ad campaign and sales would then soar.

In the 1970s, however, fundamental environmental change did impact the marketer's craft. Oil embargoes by the Organization of the Petroleum Exporting Countries (OPEC) and the Iranian hostage crisis brought globalization to the doorstep—or, more precisely, the gas tanks—of the developed nations. Runaway inflation and a deep recession constrained both consumer spending and business growth. The Nixon administration imposed price controls, which unwittingly stimulated the growth of trade spending—companies began hiking list prices to avoid future price freezes and then reimbursing customers through trade allowances. It wasn't so easy to be a marketer anymore. But it was easy, and perhaps even justified, to blame the economy rather than the marketer's capabilities.

The economy recovered in the 1980s, but the media landscape pixilated. Niche magazines, videocassette recorders (VCRs), CNN's 24-hour news cycle, MTV's quick-cut music videos, personal computers (PCs), and video games diverted and shortened customers' attention spans. But the TV networks could still deliver mass audiences, and so marketers were slow to respond to the growing number of new vehicles. Their marketing mix stayed the same, but they did reduce the 60-second TV spot to 30 seconds, running more ads, as well as experimenting with cable advertising. The fault line between environment and craft began to open under the marketers' feet.

In the 1990s, the fault split wide open. The growth of the Internet and the continued fragmentation of media made it harder than ever to reach customers en masse. There were fewer and fewer viewers for the 30-second spot. At the same time, retailers consolidated into larger and larger chains, and "big-box" competitors emerged in every segment. The power of the retailer was growing, and, as a result, spending to support retailers became a bigger and bigger expense, eventually eclipsing advertising spending in many companies. The traditional marketing model was failing, and still too many marketers continued to think in terms of yesteryear's mass media and markets.

In the new millennium, shocks and uncertainties have become a way of life, symbolized by the terrorist events of September 11, 2001, but also manifest in the world of business and commerce. Globalization, wireless communications networks, and rising information transparency have led to an increasingly mobile work-force, disruptive technologies and business models, and customers who are harder to reach and to engage than ever (think: Do Not Call Registry and new demands such as "green" products and services). Customers have many new media options—iPods, social utilities, and online video gaming, to name a few—which have changed the way they consume information and entertainment. And marketers are finding it more and more difficult to keep up with customers, let alone effectively deploy the rapidly multiplying vehicles. The fault between the marketers' environment and the craft has become a chasm.

Marketers weren't sleeping as all this change was occurring. They refined their ability to elicit insight about and from con-sumers (adopting ever-more-sophisticated segmentation strate-gies and market research techniques, for instance) and they improved their creative responses. But, these tactics alone haven't been enough to keep pace with the radical change we've experi-enced. In the past few years, marketers have come to realize that the climate requires that they rethink their craft, and today even the best of them are still grappling with the issues and searching for solutions.

This hard reality has created a tremendous amount of pressure and tension in the profession. In the sections that follow, we will explore how two forces, the same two great forces that are driv-ing the continuing reordering of our entire world, are creating and feeding this pressure and tension within marketing. We will describe how the first force, technology, has fundamentally altered the marketing landscape by empowering customers and giving rise to new media, and how the second, globalization, has created a migration of hard skills and a consolidation in many industries that has shifted the sources of corporate competitive advantage as well as growth. Also, we will discuss how these forces have raised the corporate demand for marketing efficacy and accountability to new heights, a third major source of the pressure and tension that many marketers are feeling.

EMPOWERED CUSTOMERS, SPLINTERED MEDIA

Technological change has irrevocably altered the behavior of customers. Think about the changes in customers' personal habits wrought by the revolution in technology over the past decade. How do they plan a vacation or book a business trip; shop for a new car, home appliances, or clothing; share the photos they take; choose a restaurant; listen to music; pick a book to read or a movie to watch; or decide on medical care or fill a prescription? People are approaching many, if not all, of these tasks in ways that are fundamentally different than in the past because of advances in technology. These advances also permit them almost instantaneous access to product and service information and a vast number of new buying opportunities.

Not only are customers changing their own behavior through the use of technology, they are also changing the behavior of others. They are creating communities—using Web sites, blogs, wikis, social utilities, journals, and so on—at sometimes astonishing rates. (In June 2008, for instance, Technorati, Inc., reported it was tracking over 112 million blogs, with 175,000 new blogs being created worldwide each day.)[1] They are sharing experiences, answering questions, and pooling information and opinions about everything under the sun, including your products and services.

As customers change the way they act in order to capture the benefits of new technology and embrace it to create communities that they control and where they can speak their minds, markets become more transparent and customers' buying behaviors are empowered. Customers also spend less time with traditional passive media. In short, purchase decisions are far less easily influenced by marketers and their practices than in the past. In fact without individual champions within these communities, marketers can't penetrate their borders or be heard with any degree of credibility. Likewise, segmentation becomes ever more complex as smaller and smaller cohorts spring up to replace the broad categories (such as "Women 18–40") into which marketers were able to lump customers in previous eras.

The best chief marketing officers are well aware that they must forge new relationships with empowered customers or risk having them wreak havoc on strategic plans and performance targets. Says Beth Comstock, General Electric's CMO and former president of Integrated Media at NBC Universal: "One of the biggest trends in the media space right now is that consumers are in control. And it's more than just click-the-remote capabilities or the ability to do a browse/search on the Internet. Consumers are telling us that they want to be in control of the storytelling. And, as a part of that desire, they want to engage in advertising in different ways. Marketers ignore this change at their own peril. Media companies ignore this change at their own peril. There will be times when the old kind of passive experience is going to be just right. But increasingly, consumers want to filter, they want to act, they want to be a part of the experience. And we have to be smart about it."

Ironically, the same technologies that have improved communication and connected people around the world have also created a host of new media vehicles that have made communication and connection even more problematic for marketers. The huge audiences generated by mass media have splintered, and the task of reaching the right customers at the right time in an affordable fashion has become increasingly complex.

This isn't a new trend. In 1980, in his best-selling book *The Third Wave*, futurist Alvin Toffler tracked the early decline of major newspapers and magazines, the broadcast networks, and radio in the face of growing competition. "New, de-massified media are proliferating, challenging—and sometimes even replacing—the mass media that were so dominant in all Second Wave societies," he wrote.[2] The media landscape, like consumer behavior itself, didn't change overnight, but in the quarter century since he wrote the book, Toffler's vision of the demassification of media has become a reality. For example,

- The three major TV networks (ABC, NBC, and CBS) shared 90 percent of television's prime-time audience in 1980. By April 2007, the four majors (now including Fox) had a 40 percent share, according to Nielsen Media Research.[3]
- In 1964, the average weekday newspaper readership was 80.8 percent of adults, according to Nielsen. In 2007, readership was 48 percent of adults, according to Scarborough Research.[4]
- In 1993, the average listener had the radio on 22.75 hours each week. Between fall 1993 and spring 2007, the average time spent by radio listeners dropped over 18 percent to 18.5 hours per week, according to Arbitron.[5]

Where have the mass audiences of yesterday gone? They have been diverted by a host of new entertainment and social networking vehicles. Among other things, they are watching cable and satellite television, using their DVRs to watch what they want when they want ... without commercial interruption, getting their news 24/7 from CNN. Further, when people do consume media, very often their attention is divided. For instance, a Kaiser Family Foundation survey revealed that while people are watching TV, 74 percent of them read newspapers and 66 percent use the Internet.[6]

Not only are people consuming traditional media, such as TV, radio, and print, in new ways, they continue to devote an increasing portion of their time to new media vehicles. In the United States, between 2001 and 2006, the hours consumers spent on the Internet rose 41 percent and the hours on mobile phones rose 1,264 percent.[7] Between 2005 and 2007, the unique visitors per month on social networking site MySpace grew 331 percent to 51 million, according to comScore. This growth in new forms of media is not U.S-centric; for instance, the number of mobile subscribers in China is expected to grow to 940 million by the end of 2011, and in India, the number is expected to rise to 370 million.[8] Increasingly as people study and work, they search Google and Yahoo! and blog while simultaneously instant messaging their friends and sharing iPod playlists. When they really have time to focus on entertainment, they play online video games with friends from around the world.

How has customer behavior been impacted by all of these changes? There are an infinite number of variations in the answers to that question, but let's examine the behaviors of car buyers over a 16-year period that saw a tremendous explosion in Internet usage and online media for a vivid example. Exhibit 1-1 shows an analysis of how people shopped for new cars in 1992

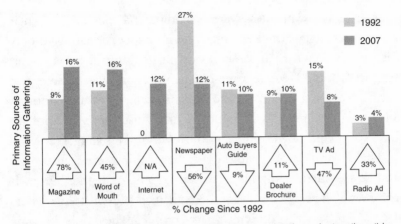

Note: Percentages do not add up to 100%. Missing categories under other and automotive articles.
Source: DoubleClick Performics Survey (Multiple Responses Allowed), CNW Research, TNS/CMR, Booz & Company Analysis

Exhibit 1-1 The Changing Influencers in Car Buying

and in 2007, revealing significant shifts among the factors that influenced their purchase decisions. The most dramatic changes can be seen in the influence of newspapers and TV, which had dropped 56 and 47 percent, respectively, and in the influence of magazines and word of mouth, which had risen 78 and 45 percent, respectively. The Internet, which did not exist so far as car buyers were concerned in 1992, had risen in just over a decade to become one of the top four influencing factors.

The shifting influencers of purchasing decisions reflect a changing landscape that you would have expected automotive marketers to negotiate with care. But when you look at how car companies were spending their advertising dollars in 2007, it is clear that they had barely shifted their advertising spend to reflect the changing degree of influence that media was having on purchase decisions. In fact, in terms of six major media sources, car companies were spending 64 percent of their advertising dollars on TV, which had an impact equating to only 23 percent on the customer's buying decision. Conversely, as seen in Exhibit 1-2, the same companies spent just 6 percent of their advertising dollars on the Internet, which accounted for an 11 percent of media's influence on the customer's decision to buy. What kind of ROI impact do those numbers suggest to you?

The technological changes that have empowered customers and demassified media have created a complex marketing environment. The challenges that these changes present to marketers are not necessarily difficult to overcome. They only become insurmountable problems when marketers cannot adjust to the new realities they represent and spend hundreds of millions of dollars in the wrong places. Marketers who do not understand

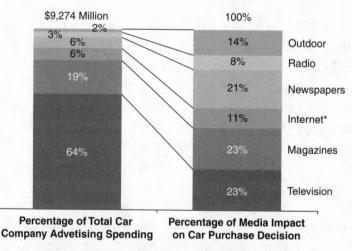

*Excludes paid search and broadband video ads
Source: TNS Media Intelligence, BIGresearch, Booz & Company Analysis

Exhibit 1-2 Car Company Media Spending vs. Influence on Consumer Behavior (2007)

the changing climatic conditions cannot make rain. As Jerri Devard, former CMO of Verizon Communications, says:

> Marketing people have always talked about the importance of single-minded focus—the single message that you disseminate to every channel and every customer. Well, this idea of communicating one message to everyone is just not going to work. Instead of spreading one message to the masses, you've got to send focused messages to many different groups—groups that have their own needs and interests. And that's also where Verizon had to carve out its revenue potential: against a base of customers who come to it for many different reasons.
>
> But I am [marketing] channel agnostic. I want to engage with people wherever they are. If they are Internet-dependent, I want to be there. If they want to pick up the phone and call us, I want to give them that opportunity. If they prefer to read and digest things, I'll send them direct mail at home. But I always want to make sure I don't overspend in some places to the detriment of others.

So the world has gotten more complicated. No longer will one message suffice for all of your customers; many customer-specific messages are required. No longer will all of your customers be watching that must-see show on TV at the same time; so your messages will have to reach them wherever they are and whenever they choose to be there. And most difficult, all of this must be achieved in a cost-effective way.

ORGANIC GROWTH, RAMPANT COMPETITION

At the same time technology has driven complexity into the marketer's job, the forces of globalization have altered the very DNA of corporate success, spawning both corporate gigantism and transforming the sources of competitive advantage. As a result of these trends, marketing itself has become a more important component of corporate performance than ever before and the pressure on marketers to produce results has increased accordingly.

In 1991, Regis McKenna declared in the *Harvard Business Review* that "marketing is everything, and everything is marketing," and it turns out that his polemic on the pervasive role of marketing was prescient.[9] In early 2004, the Association of National Advertisers (ANA) and Booz & Company launched a study to determine the relevance of marketing, marketing departments, and CMOs (although they don't always go by that moniker) in today's business climate. More than 400 respondents from over 100 companies in nine industries (auto, consumer packaged goods, financial services, health, manufacturing, professional services, retail, technology and telecom) completed a confidential survey. As Exhibit 1-3 shows, 77 percent of the marketers and 78 percent of the nonmarketers said that marketing has become

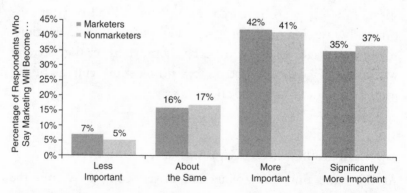

Source: ANA/Booz & Company Marketing Organization Survey 2004, ANA/Booz & Company Analysis

Exhibit 1-3 How the Importance of Marketing Has Changed over the Last Five Years

more important or significantly more important to their companies during the past five years.

We've also seen a corresponding increase in the demand for marketers from companies across the spectrum. "You can hardly go to a company now where they're not talking about building marketing capability," former P&G CMO Jim Stengel says. "I get called almost every day for advice on who can fill a job. The pace of stuff coming in about openings and needs for people with these kinds of capabilities is huge. I sit on Motorola's board, and I can see people there recognizing the power of marketing in technology."

General Electric is a notable example of a company that has responded effectively to this marketing imperative. In 2002, onetime GE CEO Jack Welch's successor, Jeff Immelt, appointed Beth Comstock as the first CMO in the then 110-year-old company's history and asked that all of the company's divisions add marketing executives to their senior teams. In the years that followed, GE applied the same energy to teaching its managers about marketing that it had to the study of Six Sigma during Jack Welch's tenure. Immelt also invited Ralph Larsen, Johnson & Johnson's former chairman and CEO, and A.G. Lafley, chairman and CEO of P&G, both heads of leading companies noted for their marketing savvy, to join GE's board of directors.[10]

Why have GE and so many other companies turned their attention to marketing? One reason is the organic growth imperative. Globalization created an unprecedented demand for scale, and many companies responded by aggressively pursuing mergers and acquisitions. Inevitably, as major companies grew larger and larger and industries consolidated, the opportunities to satisfy shareholder demands for growth in this way shrank. And, even in those sectors where opportunities do still exist, executives clearly realize that the ability to generate profitable growth through any given acquisition is limited to a two- to three-year window. At some point, the acquisition must contribute organic growth, too.

"We do need to align our marketing efforts to support and accelerate organic growth for the company," said Anne Finucane, CMO and president of Bank of America. "You can't churn customers in and out and grow a business. Once we have a customer, we work to keep him or her. We want to be their first choice and then their repeated choice. And then you need that customer to recommend our brand to family and friends. Those are the two most critical paths for driving organic growth."

Another reason for the increasing focus on marketing is that globalization has engendered a fundamental shift in the basis of our economy. Over the past several decades, it has become obvious that we are moving toward an economy that is driven by intellectual capital. Nike is a well-known example of the impact of this trend on corporate structure. The world's number one maker of athletic footwear doesn't actually manufacture athletic footwear. Its core competencies revolve around the design and marketing of footwear and the management of its supply chain; the company outsources the actual manufacturing to contractors around the world.

Nike first began pursuing its innovative strategy back in the mid-1970s, which was about the same time that America's industrial heartland began corroding into the Rust Belt. At that time the annual market-to-book multiples for the Standard & Poor's 500 Index (S&P 500) hovered around 1.0, that is, the value of these major, publicly traded companies was roughly equal to the value of their physical assets. By 1999, the height of the dot-com boom, the market-to-book multiple had risen to 5.05. Four-fifths of the value of the S&P 500 was intangible. To be sure, part of this gain was a reflection of overheated equity markets—but in 2002, after the bust, the S&P's market-to-book multiple was still at 2.735, and in the fourth quarter of 2006 the multiple was 2.812.[11] Today, the most valuable assets of the S&P 500 are still intangible. They reside in the future value of brands and customers, and organizational capabilities such as marketing prowess. So, it is no wonder that companies have turned their attention to developing those "intangible" assets.

Globalization has also fostered heightened competition in virtually every industry. Thus far, the new millennium has been an era of hypercompetition. Imported goods have been driving costs and prices down across the spectrum. Innovative new products have a shorter-than-ever window of exclusivity before copycat offerings appear. The key to delaying imitators and competing successfully in such an environment is differentiation. This differentiation can come in a variety of forms, many of which, according to our Booz & Company colleague Alex Kandybin, are intimately linked to marketing, such as benefit claims, ingredient synonymy (for example, Arm & Hammer and baking soda), and unique brand characteristics.

For instance, there may or may not be discernible quality differences between a pair of Nike's sneakers and pair of no-name Nike knock-offs, but the willingness of the typical customer to pay a premium for the pair of sneakers emblazoned with the "Swoosh" is all about the ability of Nike's marketers to create demand through the communication of the tangible and intangible benefits of its products. So, as previously mentioned, total marketing spend continues to rise, reaching estimates that range from $600 billion to as high as $1 trillion per year among U.S. companies alone. To put these figures in perspective, consider that $600 billion is a figure greater than the individual gross domestic products (GDPs) of all but 16 of the world's nations; $1 trillion is a figure greater than the individual GDPs of all but nine nations.[12]

At the same time that globalization has created an environment of hypercompetition and forced companies to bolster their marketing budgets, globalization also has been a major reason why CEOs have targeted marketing in terms of efficiency and accountability. The offshoring of manufacturing, customer service, programming, and a host of other functions was one of the primary enablers of the corporate cost-cutting boom of this decade. CEOs were able to reduce costs in virtually every function, except marketing. As the ANA's Marketing Accountability Task Force concluded:

> Management has no other place to turn for additional savings. Every other function has been Six Sigma'ed and TQM'ed [Total Quality Management] into fighting trim. Management believes operations are wound tight. The view from the corner office sees the marketing function as the last grape with any juice left unsqueezed.[13]

Ironically, the CEO's impetus to target marketing for cost cutting is exacerbated by the growing investment he or she must make in it. If you were looking at one of the top one or two expenses on your profit and loss statement, one that could very well be as high as 40 percent of sales, you would be wondering how to reduce it, too.

CORPORATE DEMAND FOR MARKETING EFFICACY AND ACCOUNTABILITY

Marketing is more important than ever. CEOs are depending on the function to connect with customers who are not only demanding more and more but also deserting the traditional paths of influence in droves. The brand, product, and service differentiation that marketers create is more and more critical to corporate performance, and CEOs are investing more and more resources to attain it. Given this scenario, you might reasonably expect that marketers would be highly valued by the senior leadership team. Yet, more often than not, members of the executive team see them in a far less favorable light.

One telling measure of the lack of corporate regard for marketers is visible in the tenure of CMOs. In 2004, global executive search firm Spencer Stuart characterized the CMO position as "fast becoming one of the riskiest jobs in North America." It discovered that only 14 percent of CMOs at the top 100 branded companies had been on the job over three years, and nearly half had less than a year in their current positions. The average CMO tenure was 22.9 months, less than two years. (By way of contrast, CEOs, whose short tenures are often in the headlines, averaged more than twice as long on the job, at 53.8 months.) In 2006, the search firm recalculated CMO tenure; after two years it had remained virtually the same, rising less than two weeks to 23.2 months. In 2007, CMO tenure rose more significantly, but still, at 26.8 months, there was little to cheer about.[14]

The rate of restructurings among the marketing function, as shown in Exhibit 1-4, is equally telling. In 2004, an ANA/Booz & Company study found that fully 70 percent of companies in nine industries had restructured their marketing functions

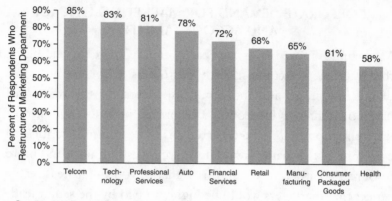

Source: ANA/Booz & Company Analysis

Exhibit 1-4 Organizational Restructurings in Marketing, 2001–2004

over the previous three years. Among professional service firms, telecoms, and technology companies—sectors that were particularly hard hit when the irrational exuberance of the late 1990s drained away—the figure rose to over 80 percent.

Why are CMOs dropping like flies and marketing organizations experiencing such chaos? One major reason is that there is an often fatal disconnect between the objectives of CMOs and CEOs. The same study found that marketing was not aligned with the CEO's agenda at more than half of all companies surveyed. While CEOs fret about growing and adapting to change, CMOs are focused on devising guidelines and proffering tactical advice.

According to the Conference Board's *CEO Challenge 2006* report, these were the top four priorities for CEOs:

- Sustained and steady top-line growth
- Profit growth
- Consistent execution of strategy by top management
- Speed, flexibility, adaptability to change

In contrast, our study found that marketers are focused more around these issues:

- Setting and maintaining branding guidelines (83 percent)
- Counseling divisions (52 percent)
- Sharing best practices (52 percent)

Driving the CEO agenda and driving innovation garnered only a 37 percent and 35 percent response from marketers, ranking last on their priority lists.[15] Granted, our survey sample was probably skewed toward corporate marketing managers, who are charged with standardizing brand investments, but the fact remains that less than half of the respondents indicated that the issues that keep CEOs awake at night are at the top of their agendas. And, you must wonder how anyone can be a marketer and not have growth, or better yet, profitable growth, at the top of his or her agenda?

Central to this disconnect is the inability of marketers to measure their results and account for them in the financial language of profit, loss, and return on investment. The leading finding in a 2007 study by the CMO Council was that "nearly three-quarters of the C-suite executives surveyed consider the marketing organization 'highly influential and strategic in the enterprise.' At the same time, nearly two-thirds also say that their top marketers don't provide adequate ROI with which to gauge marketing's true performance."[16]

Another 2007 study, conducted by Financial Executives International, found that only 10 percent of senior financial executives had confidence in marketing's ability to forecast the impact of its actions on sales. And, marketers don't have all that much more confidence in themselves. A 2006 ANA study found that only 25 percent of marketers felt they had sufficient ability to predict their impact on sales.[17]

In fact, marketing's inability to measure performance is one of the biggest sources of friction between CMOs and CEOs today. The Booz & Company study with the ANA found that more than half of the respondents (51 percent) said that the difficulty in measuring performance is a key reason for pressure on the marketing department. "There is no consistent definition of ROI," noted one respondent. "[We] are using rule of thumb guidelines on a good day . . . there is just no way around it, we have to get better fast."

MEETING THE MARKETER'S CHALLENGE

A marketing ROI capability, when properly developed, holds the key to relieving the pressures and tensions that marketers are currently experiencing, as well as providing the insight that marketers need to connect with customers, optimize their performance, maximize their contribution to their businesses, and rightfully earn a place at the leadership table. It also has the power to dispel one of marketing's most pervasive and dangerous myths—the myth that marketing is an art, not a science.

Like all enduring myths, this one has some basis in reality. It is true that the ability to capture customer attention and influence buying behaviors does require both insight and creativity. But nevertheless, it is a myth. Unlike art, marketing is not undertaken for its own sake; unlike art, creative insight and impact are not the purpose of the endeavor. Marketing is undertaken to create customer connection, brand and product differentiation, sales, and profitable growth. These are business goals, and a marketing ROI capability enables their achievement. The following are the major benefits of building such a capability:

Drives profitable organic growth. Marketers have always been focused on organic growth through identification, acquisition, and retention of customers (with the exception of those misguided practitioners who swallow the "art myth" and chase creativity awards). Without measurement, however, it is impossible to say if marketing events—whether they are promotions, price changes, or advertisements—are actually contributing to such growth. Marketing ROI can be an engine of organic growth. Measurement enables marketers to quantify their results and shift their resources to those vehicles and creative campaigns that are generating growth. Marketing ROI drives smart spending and allows companies to earn the best returns on their marketing dollars.

Aligns marketing with corporate objectives and creates accountability. As described above, too often marketers are running into self-imposed barriers created by the misalignment of their efforts with the business objectives of their companies. CMOs must be able to make sound business cases that are capable of justifying ever-increasing marketing spends, and CEOs and CFOs are less and less willing to accept soft-headed reasoning, such as "raising awareness," in support of those cases. They want to know how the spending will support their goals and what returns they can expect. Further, marketers must be able to determine if those returns actually materialized and use that knowledge to support resource allocation targeted toward campaigns and vehicles that work.

Marketing ROI is the basis of a capability that enables marketers to provide the answers to those questions. It encompasses the processes needed to realign their actions to strategic objectives, to design events and allocate resources that support those objectives, and to communicate their accomplishments to both their peers and their leaders. In fact, if the capability is fully developed, it will yield the knowledge that other functions can use to improve their own performance, as well. In this case, marketing can assume the strategic role within a business that management experts, such as the late Peter Drucker, have long suggested it should hold.

Enables enhanced creativity. Experimentation is critical in marketing or any other creative process. Achieving success in today's ever-changing environment demands it. Marketers must learn how to respond to today's empowered customers and how to cope with splintered media. They must be able to experiment in order to gain the insight they require to connect with customers and to test and refine their creative responses.

If marketers can't measure the results of their experiments, this unavoidable process of trial and error is left to intuition and chance. "Hmm," the marketer muses, "I allocated 50 percent of my spend to TV last year, but everybody's talking about buzz marketing. I'll cut TV by five points and put it there." A year passes and sales are flat. What should the marketer do now? (By the way, this may sound overly simplistic, but remember that 30 to 50 percent of the executives with whom we meet cannot even place a figure on their total marketing spend.)

Marketing ROI, on the other hand, can be the driving force in a virtuous learning cycle. It imposes efficiency and rigor on the creative experimentation that lies at the heart of the discipline, and in measuring the results of those experiments, it creates the knowledge that marketers need to decide which experiments work and which don't. And if you don't know if an edgy, creative ad works, what are the chances it will stay on air or online? Further, the ability to measure marketing results in a standardized way is necessary to create the transparency that CEOs and executive boards are demanding. This transparency facilitates marketing's credibility within the organization, and when it illuminates profitable sales growth, it also generates support for the most creative work.

Represents a new competitive advantage. In the ever-changing business world, you can't stand pat—inevitably, you will lose. You can wait for someone else to discover the way, but in that case, you will always be an also-ran. Paradoxically, the best odds are to embrace risk and pursue, and, perhaps, even create change.

Marketing ROI requires change and hard work, but it represents a prime opportunity to jump ahead of the competition. The fact that it is a capability that is not easily built also means it is one that is not easily copied. There are companies that are already leaders in this race, but the science and the technology that support this capability are continuously changing, and as we write this few have put all of the pieces together. This is a race that is still being run and can be won.

MEETING THE NEW MEDIA CHALLENGE WITH ROI

One of the great profitability challenges facing today's marketers is how to make optimal use of the vast array of new media vehicles that have recently appeared and continue to emerge. The challenge stems from two conditions: first, there are a host of new media metrics that can be adopted, but no one knows exactly which to use, and the metrics are not yet standardized. ROI can help solve both of these problems.

The first problem with new media is deciding what to measure. In traditional media, measures are well established. TV uses gross rating points (GRPs); print uses audited subscriber and readership numbers. However,

Continued

---

in new media, such as search, mobile, and video game advertising, there are a plethora of potential measures. Online media companies, for instance, offer marketers:

- Impression metrics such as page views or visit time
- Message metrics such as ad likability, ad engagement, and message relevance
- Attitudinal metrics such as top of mind awareness, brand imagery, and brand favorability
- Behavioral response metrics such as click-throughs, opt-in registrations, or pass-along rates
- Transactional metrics such as number of sales per session

But which of these metrics should marketers use, and in what circumstances? As yet, comprehensive answers to that question remain unclear.

Secondly, in new media, even the simplest of results can be a source of confusion because universally accepted standards are not in place. Most notably, Nielsen and comScore are the two major market research firms tracking "eyeballs" on the Internet, yet they are counting eyeballs in different ways, and therefore reporting varied results. So, marketers can't be sure exactly how many people saw their banner ads, and thus, disputes around payment arise, results are obscured; and because marketers cannot establish a sound, or at least consistent, basis for their spending, they are reluctant to invest in new media vehicles at the very time that many of their customers are migrating to them.

As with any other more traditional media, a good way to cut through the confusion is to begin to reduce the noise by focusing on well-defined marketing objectives and the measurement of ROI. Cost, and the incremental volume produced by that investment, are easily measured for many popular new media vehicles. Click-through-to-purchase on a banner ad on a Web site or mobile text message can be measured exactly. You run an online campaign, you see if your sales increase, and then use the results as the basis for making decisions on future spending.

Not all new media lends itself to easy ROI calculation. Like billboards and image print ads, blogging and social networking can be hard to monetize. But even in these cases, the interactive nature of new media offers a better environment to calculate ROI because customers' actions can be tracked. Marketers who build their ROI capability can take advantage of these benefits and get a handle on new media.

A competitive advantage that enhances profitability, creativity, and accountability—we recognize that this is an ambitious claim. So, before we start to explore the components of a marketing ROI capability and how they come together to deliver these benefits, we need to examine how ROI transforms the effectiveness of the marketing cycle and explain why it is the metric that you should focus on at this time. These are the subjects of Chapter 2.

Chapter 2

Marketing and ROI Microeconomics

here is widespread confusion, even among marketers, about what marketing does and how well it does it. The marketing functions in the companies that we visit are all structured differently and assigned varying spans of authority and responsibility. Marketing also resides at different levels within different businesses. It has strategic, operational, and tactical roles, which may or may not be present in a specific company. Further, the very definition of marketing is elusive; there is no accepted standard. It is no wonder that it can be tough to get your arms around marketing, let alone make it pay.

The eminent management writer Peter Drucker unwittingly contributed to the confusion around marketing when he reduced the purpose of a business to the logically elegant phrase: *to create a customer*. In doing so, he elevated marketing, which is all about creating and connecting with customers, to "a central dimension of the entire business."[1] Drucker thus set the stage for Regis McKenna's "marketing is everything and everyone is a marketer" argument. This may be true in the macro sense when speaking of the purpose of business, but it blurs the distinctive role of marketing as a science and profession.

The "blind men and the elephant" syndrome also inhibits a practical understanding of marketing. As in the old Indian story in which six blind men touch different parts of an elephant and then describe it in wildly disparate ways, the practitioners and advocates of marketing specialties tend to see their piece of the discipline as the most important piece. Strategists tend to see marketing in terms of competitive positioning and segmentation; market researchers see it as insight into customers; advertising gurus emphasize finding the big idea. All of these facets are important, but understanding a piece of something is not the same as having a holistic understanding.

Demystifying marketing and gaining a working understanding of the marketing process is the first step to understanding the role of ROI. Drucker's definition is a good place to start. Marketing's purpose, like that of a business, is to create a customer. Marketers do this by establishing differentiation in the marketplace and stimulating demand. Marketing is not the only function in a business trying to create differentiation and demand, but it is the one function that is solely dedicated to that task, and in the best of times, it is the one that approaches it most comprehensively.

While marketers create differentiation in many ways, the best marketing practitioners approach their work as a deliberative process. As seen in Exhibit 2-1, this process is composed of four stages: insight, creation, communication, and measurement.

An effective marketing process always begins with an insight into the needs and desires of a target audience. Insights can come from anywhere. Perhaps too often, they have been intuitive—a gut feeling about what customers want or a personal preference that the marketer believes customers will share. This type of insight is vulnerable, for even the most experienced or intuitively canny marketer is wrong sometimes. Insights can also be more empirical, derived from the comments of focus groups, the results of consumer surveys, or more fact-based sources such as

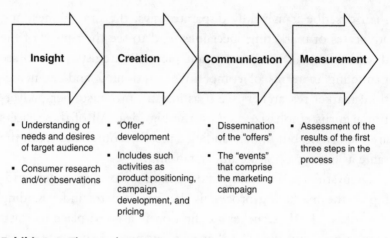

Insight	Creation	Communication	Measurement
■ Understanding of needs and desires of target audience ■ Consumer research and/or observations	■ "Offer" development ■ Includes such activities as product positioning, campaign development, and pricing	■ Dissemination of the "offers" ■ The "events" that comprise the marketing campaign	■ Assessment of the results of the first three steps in the process

Exhibit 2-1 The Marketing Process

the direct observation of customer behavior or the measurement of their responses to a marketer's offer. When these intuitions and observations are filtered and synthesized, they yield a point of view—an insight—regarding customers' wants and needs.

In the next stage of the process, marketers transform their insights into what they hope and presumably believe is a compelling offer. This is a creative undertaking that can be initiated and carried out at strategic, operational, and tactical levels within a business. Marketers might create a corporate value proposition or positioning statement based on their insights. They might reposition a single brand, sponsor a sporting event, repackage a product, create an ad campaign, or institute a new pricing structure. Whatever the focus of marketers' efforts, during the creation stage, they are seeking to produce an offer that is capable of establishing differentiation, attracting new customers, and/or enhancing the connection between customers and the products and services sold by their companies.

Communication, the third stage in the process, is the dissemination of the marketer's offers. Marketers disseminate offers through *events*, the atom of marketing—its single, indivisible unit of analysis. In order to create events, marketers must choose a vehicle, a time period, and a target audience. These are the fundamental building blocks of an event. Often, events are thematically interrelated but also discrete. In other words, each ad in an ad campaign is a separate event. Each sampling promotion that a liquor company conducts in bars around the country is an event. Every time a marketer communicates to customers, whether via a television commercial, rebate program, in-store display, banner ad, sponsorship, or direct-marketing mailer, it is an event. Thus, marketers at a major company will communicate with customers and disseminate their offers through thousands, and sometimes tens of thousands, of events each year.

The final stage in the marketer's process is measurement, which is also the source of ROI and provides much of the impetus for creating marketing that successfully connects with customers and corporate goals. Measurement is the way that marketers discover how accurate their insights, effective their creative offers, and well chosen their events have been. Typically, measurement is problematic for marketers. In the worst cases, of which there are many, they can determine the outcomes of their events only in the broadest metrics such as the company's annual sales volume and net income. Far less often, but with far more advantage, outcomes can be measured very specifically, such as the ROI that a coupon generates at a specific retail location. But no matter what level of analytical rigor is applied, this is where marketers, and their bosses, determine how well they have done their jobs.

McDonald's Corporation's classic "You deserve a break today" advertising campaign is one of marketing's classic success stories, as well as a good example for illustrating this concept of measurement in action. McDonald's, which grew from a single California drive-in restaurant in 1940 to a 228-outlet franchise chain by 1960, didn't have a marketing department or a national advertising program until 1967. Five years later, it was one of the most prolific advertisers in the country.

In 1969, the national ad agency Needham, Harper & Steers won the fast-food chain's account on the basis of a proposal by an account executive named Keith Reinhard. Reinhard "invaded the McDonald's stores with our research people," and he constructed his first campaign for the company around the idea that going to McDonald's was like escaping to an "island of enjoyment." Fatefully, however, just two weeks before the campaign's production deadline, billboards that advertised A&W Restaurants, Inc., as "islands of pleasure" began to pop up.

As the entire Needham agency scrambled to come up with something new, Reinhard went back to the market research and emerged with an insight. "Women would complain how they would have to plan for dinner every night," he later said. "They used the word *break* a lot of time. That's how 'You deserve a break today' was an insight into the consumer, gained from the consumer. Did I write that line? Not really. I got it from the consumer."

It was actually Al Klatt, the head of the Needham's advertising review board, who came up with the key phrase. Reinhard inserted it in what was left of the song from the ill-fated island campaign, creating the line: "You deserve a break today, so get up and get away ... to McDonald's." With its offer in place, McDonald's was ready to communicate with American families, its target audience. In 1971, it rolled out the campaign on broadcast television—the vehicle that was clearly the best way to reach that audience in that era. Each national airing of a "break today" commercial was an event.

Measuring the impact of the new campaign, at least in aggregate, was easy for McDonald's in that era of mass markets; same-store sales across the system jumped as soon as the national campaign was launched. In 1973, *Time* magazine devoted a cover story to the chain's explosive growth, proclaiming, "The company's relentless advertising campaign ($50 million budgeted this year) has made the McDonald's jingle, *You Deserve a Break Today*, almost as familiar as *The Star-Spangled Banner*." It also reported that McDonald's had surpassed the U.S. Army "as the nation's biggest dispenser of meals." Systemwide sales, which also include the addition of new stores and other factors not entirely attributable to the campaign, rose from $587 million in 1970 to more than $1 billion in 1972 and $3 billion in 1976. The "You deserve a break today" campaign, by the way, took the fifth spot on *Advertising Age*'s list of the top 100 advertising campaigns of the last century, and Keith Reinhard went on to become the chairman and CEO of DDB Needham.[2]

ROI TRANSFORMS THE MARKETING PROCESS

Marketing is easier to understand when it is stripped down to its basic process, but the way in which the process is commonly executed often adds significant uncertainty and risk to the function.

First, and far too often, the marketer's attention and energy are front-loaded in terms of the process. In other words, marketers spend a lot of their time generating insight and creating offers, but most of them haven't thought as deeply about the final two stages—communication and measurement. They tend to depend too heavily on the traditional "proven" vehicles to disseminate their creative offers. As for the measurement stage, it is often ignored altogether. As we've seen, many marketers simply don't know the specific outcomes of their events. Typically, they do have a sense of outcomes as reflected in high-level corporate metrics such as revenue and net income. But these marketers are reduced to guessing about whether their events are driving these numbers and, if so, which of their events have been effective and why.

Second, on those occasions when specific events are measured, the results are not applied toward improving future events. In other words, the data is gathered, but it gathers dust. It is not transformed into the working knowledge that can be used to create a better connection to customers and thus better results the next time around. In part, that's because many marketing professionals are simply unaware of the data and the analytical capabilities that reside within their own companies. Recently, a Booz & Company team met with senior marketers in a major financial services company who declared that their company had no modeling capacity whatsoever. But in later meetings, executives in corporate strategy introduced the team to the PhDs in the "analytics group," who, as it turned out, had been building models aimed at predicting customer response for some time. The biggest issue the organization faced was that the broader organization did not know about this capability and was not utilizing this resource.

An effective ROI-based approach, as illustrated in Exhibit 2-2, can help marketers put the "measure" in the measurement stage. Further, by using it to apply more rigor to the other three stages, they can use it to "close" the marketing process and turn it into a loop of learning and continuous improvement.

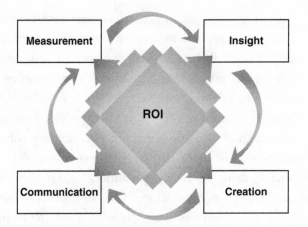

Exhibit 2-2 The ROI Marketing Loop

When ROI is utilized properly, it can transform the marketing process. Logically, its first appearance in the process comes in the measurement stage. It enables marketers to determine the outcomes of their events in terms of profitability. In the late 1990s, grocery retailer Kroger's "Big buy, big sell," a deep-discount promotion held across the chain, provided a good example of the role that ROI plays in this loop. Several large consumer products companies participated in these promotions. The cost of entry was very high, several million dollars per event. Nevertheless, the promotion was very popular with consumer product manufacturers (so popular that Kroger was able to auction the promotions across categories and manufacturers), because invariably, the chainwide displays created a huge bump in sales volume. The aggregate measures "felt" good to the marketers, but when the profitability of the event was measured and analyzed, they were dismayed to discover that at the same time the profitability of the Kroger account was falling.

Once the profitability of an event has been established, it can be linked back and applied to each of the previous three stages of the loop. Because ROI is a direct measure of real-world consumer response (as opposed to a marketer's intuition or a consumer's statement of intention), it is a highly valuable source of insight. Marketers can use it to refine their previous insights and to gain new insights into consumers in two primary ways. First, ROI provides insight into the effectiveness of the vehicle that the marketer is using to reach consumers. These are especially valuable insights in a time when new, unproven vehicles are emerging with ever-greater frequency. Second, ROI provides insight into the effectiveness of the marketer's offer. Having the right vehicle and right offer are critical to maximizing marketing profitability. In the case of Kroger, the data naturally led one of the company participants to question the effectiveness of the event. Two insights were revealed: first, the auction process had driven the cost of the promotion beyond a viable level, and second, Kroger's shoppers were waiting until the "Big buy, big sell" promotions to purchase their favorite brands and then "pantry loading"—buying large quantities that would last them until the next big sale. Together, these two factors were eroding the profitability of the company's brands.

ROI plays a similarly beneficial role in the creation stage of the marketing process. Some marketers mistakenly view the measurement of profitability as a potential constraint on their creativity. They think that if they must calculate the return of every event, they will not be allowed to experiment or conduct events that have a long-term focus such as building brand awareness. But the fact is that profitability *creates* freedom. When profitability rises, existing budgets can be stretched further and future budgets get bigger. There is more inclination to really experiment—to push the envelope of creativity in both offers and vehicles—when you can measure results in a meaningful way. Further, when there is a quantitative basis for judging the quality of marketing creativity, it is less likely that a boss or an advertising guru can dominate or bias the creative process.

So, be creative *and* measure what happens. If it works, do more of it. If it doesn't work, go back and be creative again. As Procter & Gamble's former CMO Jim Stengel says, "It's important to have extremely strong discipline and extremely high creativity. If you put those two together, it's magic."[3] In the Kroger example, the company's responses were to stop participating in the "Big buy, big sell" promotions and design new promotions of their own that featured smaller discounts and higher returns.

Finally, ROI has a positive impact on the communication stage of the marketer's process in several ways. As the number of vehicles for reaching customers increases, the dissemination of marketing becomes more and more challenging. ROI is a viable way of determining whether these vehicles are working as promised and how to allocate the marketing budget among them. Also, because events are often planned months in advance, timely ROI measurement can enable marketers to make midcourse adjustments. In the Kroger case, the consumer products manufacturer often used the portion of the budget previously allocated to "Big buy, big sell" to run the lower discount promotions more frequently. The company closed the loop when it measured the results and discovered that the lower discounts offered during these new events were more profitable than the "Big buy, big sell" promotion and that their increased frequency stimulated volume growth.

When ROI is applied in each stage and closes the process, the resulting loop enables marketers to gain more control over their work and their spending. They are better able to develop marketing that effectively creates customer connects and differentiation, and allocate more of their spending to the places where they have accomplished those goals.

DEFINING ROI

ROI is calculated in many different ways, so it is important to create a common definition. The easiest way to calculate return on investment is to divide revenue by cost. But that is too simplistic for the purposes of marketers. As legions of dismayed marketers, and other managers, too, have already discovered, revenue does not always translate into profits. This is why ROI is more relevant when it is calculated in terms of profit.

We inject profit into the ROI by adding variable contribution margin (VCM), or variable profit per volume unit, to the equation. VCM is the profit earned on each unit sold. It is calculated by adding the variable component of cost of goods sold (COGS)—which includes material, packaging, direct labor, and so on—and other variable costs across the P&L report, such as the cost of shipping the product to different locales, sales commissions, and so on, and then subtracting them from the price for which the product or service was sold. (Fixed costs, such as land, interest, and any other costs that remain stable for approximately six months or more, are ignored in this formula.)

To calculate the ROI of an event, we multiply VCM (the profit earned on a single unit) by the incremental volume (that is, the number of units sold in excess of the normal sales volume) that the event delivers and then subtract the cost of the event.

The resulting figure is divided by the cost of the event, translating the figure into percentage. The formula looks like this:

$$\text{ROI} = \frac{(\text{VCM} \times \text{Incremental Volume}) - \text{Total Spend}}{\text{Total Spend}}$$

We can illustrate how this works with the simple example of a series of sampling events run in a chain of wholesale warehouse clubs by a manufacturer of frozen egg rolls. The list price per unit of the egg rolls is $5.00 and their total variable cost is $2.00 (including $1.50 in the variable component of cost of goods sold and other variable costs of $0.50 per unit). Subtracting the cost from the list price tells us that the manufacturer's average VCM is $3.00.

Typically, the manufacturer sells 150,000 boxes of egg rolls through the clubs each month, but in the month during which the sampling runs, it sells 250,00 units. Subtracting the base volume of 150,000 from the consumed volume of 250,000 gives us an incremental volume of 100,000 units.

The sampling events run for four hours each in all 500 of the chain's locations. The manufacturer pays the chain a flat fee of $50,000 to run the events and spends another $60,000 for expenses such as the workers staffing the stations, signage, and so on. Total spend is $110,000. Now, what's the ROI of the entire event?

$$\frac{(\$3.00\ \text{VCM} \times 100,000\ \text{Incremental Units}) - \$110,000\ \text{Total Spend}}{\$110,000\ \text{Total Spend}} = \textit{172.7\% ROI}$$

Of course, in the real world, our egg roll maker would be running many events simultaneously, such as print ads, direct mail coupons, Internet banners, and TV spots, and the sales produced by those events would be mixed up with the sales generated by the sampling events. So, determining the ROI is actually much more complex and requires a sophisticated analytics. But, the principle behind this profit-based method of calculating ROI remains the same. And once the data streams and engine are in place, marketers can accurately calculate their ROI down to the granular level of single events. They can also compare their results across events and vehicles. This enables marketers to maximize the profits derived from their budgets by directing their spending to the events that produce the highest ROIs (or the next best event, if their highest ROI event costs more than their budgets). In other words, once marketers know the ROI of their events, they can get the microeconomics of marketing ROI working in their favor.

THE MICROECONOMIC EFFECT OF MARKETING ROI

Microeconomics sounds like a forbidding topic to many marketers, so let's start by describing marketing ROI in the more accessible terms of the great American pastime of baseball. An ad campaign like McDonald's "You deserve a break today" was clearly a home run, but the fast-food giant also has had its share of strikeouts over the years. In May 1996, for example, McDonald's launched its newly developed Arch Deluxe adult fare. Unfortunately, the $100 million advertising campaign—"The burger with the grown-up taste"—was a flop, and comparable store sales dropped. Like batters in baseball, however, marketers don't need to hit a homerun every time they come to the plate in order to be extraordinarily successful. What they really need to do is pick up an additional base hit here and there. Extra hits add up to extra runs.

At its essence, the ability of marketers to calculate the ROI of events creates a source of knowledge and insight that is an impetus for performance improvement. As such, it is a very effective mechanism for producing those extra hits. All marketing events, whether their purpose is to make consumers aware of your product, to induce someone who uses another brand to try yours, or to reinforce the good taste of a loyal customer, are designed to stimulate changes in customer behavior. Each event has a variety of measurable outcomes, including an ROI (which we now know how to calculate). In order to improve the ROI of your total marketing spend, which is the sum of the profitability of all of these discrete events, you need more base hits. In other words, the best way to make more money in the long term is to raise the overall profitability of your events by replacing low ROI events with events that have greater returns.

Another way of visualizing this is to plot the ROIs of a company's marketing events by the frequency with which they occur, as shown in Exhibit 2-3. This produces a distribution curve.

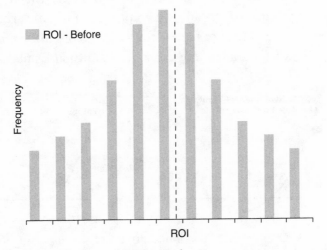

Exhibit 2-3 Distribution of ROI—"Before"

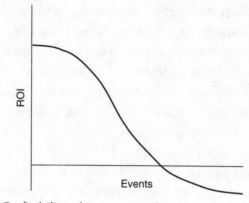

Exhibit 2-4 Profitability of Events—"Before"

A few of the events on this curve would be "You deserve a break today" homeruns, a few would be "The burger with the grown-up taste" three-pitch strikeouts, but the vast majority of events would fall somewhere between those two extremes.

In redrawing this curve to chart each individual event according to its ROI, as in Exhibit 2-4, it becomes clear which events produced positive results and which produced negative results.

Now, if you redesign or replace the losing events, like our clients did at Kroger, the shifts curve upward, as shown in Exhibit 2-5.

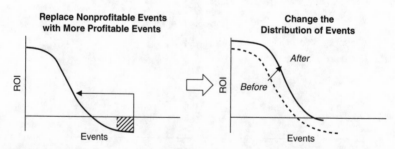

Exhibit 2-5 Changing the Distribution of Events by Replacing the Nonprofitable Events with More Profitable Events

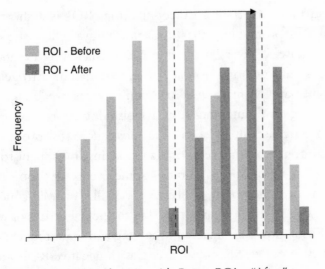

Exhibit 2-6 Tighter Distribution with Better ROI—"After"

And when the view is flipped back to reflect the view shown in Exhibit 2-3, the marketing results produce a tighter curve featuring higher overall ROI, as seen in Exhibit 2-6. The salient point here is the same as before: you can raise the overall ROI of your marketing spend by doing more of the "good" events and less of the "bad" events. This is the microeconomic effect of marketing ROI.

WHY ROI?

It's worth noting that all theoretical arguments for the benefits of ROI contain a major assumption. The assumption is that ROI is the primary measure that marketers should use in order to improve their outcomes and become more accountable for their results. That bears further exploration.

First, it is important to recognize that ROI is a short-term measure of profitability that does not always reflect the entire business case for every marketing event. Marketing events have different purposes, and not all of them are designed to generate an immediate profit. Some marketing events are designed to create long-term outcomes such as bolstering awareness or stimulating purchase intent. Even the most successful products go through rough patches requiring a marketing investment to reinvigorate or reposition the brand. Some events are good public relations or done purely to foster goodwill. If a well-conceived Super Bowl ad did not pay for itself in the next few days or weeks, it could still prove invaluable in the long run in getting exposure for a new product. So, not all events with negative ROIs are bad events nor should you replace every event with a negative ROI event with a different event that boasts a higher ROI.

With that said, it is also just as important to acknowledge that marketers cannot optimize their performance and be accountable for their results unless they can define and justify the purpose of every event as well as have some way to measure whether that purpose has been achieved. Nine-tenths of all marketing events have measurable, short-term ROIs, and you should be able maximize the profitability of those events. (The remaining 10 percent may not be measurable in terms of ROI, but nevertheless, you must be able to measure their results in some tangible way in order to maximize their "returns," too.)

Take General Electric's long-running image campaign built around the tagline "We bring good things to life." Phil Dusenberry, who went on to become chairman of BBDO North America, created it in 1979 to establish the positive impact that GE's many products and services had in consumers' lives.[4] If this campaign worked, which we presume it did given the fact that

GE did not replace it for 24 years, GE's marketers should have seen a short-term ROI as well as a long-term one. At least a few of the consumers who were newly aware about GE's role in their lives should have bought something. Further, GE's marketers should have been able to measure the ROI of this image campaign and compare it to the ROI of previous image campaigns. And, if they didn't see anything happening at all in the short term, they should have been questioning the long-term effectiveness of the campaign. The bottom line: an event that does not create a new customer or sale in the short term will very likely not be a viable profit-generating campaign in the future.

Second, ROI is not the *only* useful metric within the marketing universe. There is a great deal of debate around which marketing metric is "best." Net present value (NPV), return on customer (ROC), and customer lifetime value (CLV) are a few of these. None of them, including ROI, is a silver bullet.

ROI, however, should be one of the primary metrics on which every marketing organization is focusing. For starters, ROI is viable, accurate, and relatively easy to determine. These are major advantages in a business function that in many industries and companies is still in the early stages of measuring its outcomes. Marketers need to walk before they run, and ROI is a measure that can get them up on their feet.

Next, because ROI is a short-term measure, there are fewer unknowns floating around in its algorithms. In IMD professor Phil Rosenzweig's 2007 book, *The Halo Effect*, he points out that many of the most widely accepted and adopted expert conclusions about long-term business success are fundamentally flawed by errors in research, such as identifying factors as *contributing* to corporate success when they are, in fact, attributions *based* on that success. In fact, when Rosenzweig studied the "excellent" companies that

Tom Peters and Bob Waterman studied in *In Search of Excellence*, he found in the 5 years after the study, 30 of the 35 companies had profits decline. Likewise, of the 17 "visionary" companies that Jim Collins and Jerry Porras identified as significantly outperforming the S&P 500 in their *Built to Last* study, the stock price of 9 companies did not keep up with the S&P 500 in the 5 years after the study; 10 had not kept up 10 years after the study. The logical conclusion, declares Rosenzweig, is that we actually know very little about long-term business success.[5] Certainly, if this true for business at large, it is also true in marketing.

By necessity, there are so many assumptions in long-term measures of marketing success that the accuracy of analytical results is low. As former Verizon CMO Jerri DeVard points out, "We used to talk a lot about the lifetime value of a customer, but no one has that luxury anymore. It's presumptuous to think you're going to have a customer for life." There are also significant unknowns inherent in long-term measures, such as estimates as to the future cash flow of a customer, which may or may not prove out. Thus, the longer the metric's timeline, the harder it becomes to distinguish good events from bad ones.

So, no matter what other measures marketers add to their dashboards, there will always be a place for ROI. If you are measuring the lifetime or return on customers, for instance, ROI can tell you if and when your customers' behaviors begin to change.

Lastly, as trite as it might sound, has any marketer ever been fired for improving the profitability of the function? ROI is a precise measure of profitability that is tied directly to customer behavior and links marketers to the economic foundation of the business. Further, it is a measure that CEOs, CFOs, and boards of directors can get their arms around. If the profitability of marketing is rising, something good is happening.

THE CMO's DASHBOARD

The best and, we've noticed, the least-stressed CMOs always seem to have marketing dashboards. These dashboards gather key marketing metrics into a convenient format. When they are well designed, they display measures that portray a well-rounded picture of long-term and short-term brand health and marketing performance.

The utility of a dashboard is predicated on the quality of its measures. Properly chosen measures are a direct reflection of the priorities of the individual company and parameters of the industries in which it competes. Obviously, these metrics must also be accurately calculated. Typically, measures in a marketing dashboard will include quantitative measures such as ROI, attitudinal measures such as awareness, behavioral measures such as share of wallet, and so on.

Dashboards help marketers understand and share the results of their work. They also assist marketers in the difficult task of framing the *right* questions about their performance. As Keith Pardy, Nokia Corporation's senior vice president of strategic marketing, brand management, and consumer relationships, says: "We really focus on the marketing dashboard of 30-plus metrics that we look at on a quarterly basis. We set precise targets for these measures and look at them holistically. And we ask ourselves, 'What's happening with our brand preference scores? What's happened to our user base? Have we brought in new people? What's happening to our retention? How much money are we investing in fixed marketing versus working media?'"

SO, WHERE ARE ALL THE ROI MARKETERS?

Here is the question that naturally occurs at this point: if marketing ROI is so clearly beneficial, why isn't everybody already doing it? The answer is that marketing ROI is not just a number, it is a complex capability that requires substantial effort to develop and master. When marketers consider the requirements of this capability, many become discouraged as they find out the following things:

- *The data that they need to calculate ROI are not readily available.* The biggest impediment to success in marketing is the lack of reliable, consistent data. This is ironic in a time when companies are drowning in data; nevertheless, it is a fact. Filling the data pool needed to enable targeted analytics and fuel this capability can be time consuming—in some cases, it takes several years—and can also require developing entirely new data sources, as we've seen with various new media technologies and vehicles such as digital video recorders and online advertising.

- *They can't create and routinize the ROI calculation.* There is no black box that simply spits out the answers to all marketing ROI questions. The analytical needs of ROI marketers are highly dependent on the business they are in and the vehicles they are using to reach customers. The capability requires highly sophisticated analytics and people who can formulate the algorithms that will yield the answers. Typically, the expertise needed to develop these analytics and the algorithms on which they depend is not readily available within the existing marketing function, and in many companies it is not available at all. Further, the calculations must be routinized. In many companies, there are thousands or even tens of thousands of marketing events each year. If the calculations used to analyze them are not routinized and capable of producing comparable answers, the utility of the answers they yield will be severely limited.

- *They can't transform ROI into working knowledge and deploy it.* Calculating the outcome of an event is only the first competence in the capability. In order to transform that outcome into improvement, marketers must be able to determine the factors that caused the outcome and manipulate those causes to create improved better customer connections and outcomes in the future. New media vehicles are particularly challenging in this regard, because no one is entirely sure how they drive consumer response, and their cost and payout models are not yet well defined. Nevertheless, marketers must develop fact-based rules of thumb or predictive models as well as the processes and people who are willing to and capable of using them. Knowledge without action is an exercise in futility.

- *They can't muster the organizational support needed.* Developing a marketing ROI capability usually requires substantial investments and behavioral changes, both of which can be difficult to obtain in most companies. Marketers who work in companies whose cultures and/or senior leaders do not place a high value on fact-based management and accountability will find it difficult to establish and develop the capability. There are also those companies that disagree with Peter Drucker's conception of marketing and place little value on the function itself. Marketers who are marginalized and have little authority within their companies will find it difficult, too.

- *They are unwilling to undertake the journey.* The final barrier to the marketing ROI capability is marketers themselves. The ability to measure outcomes creates transparency and accountability. Many marketers embrace these benefits, but inevitably, some marketers see them in a less positive light. The latter group, often reacting to the pressures of the moment, depends on the murkiness around marketing to hide negative outcomes and protect themselves. The problem, of course, is that this is a shortsighted tactic; the murkiness also forces these marketers to drive blindly ahead and eventually, they will crash. (However, this tactic can work for managers who are being rotated out of the function or jobs within the function quickly, which is another reason why objective methods of marketing success are so important.)

These barriers to using marketing ROI to better connect to customer and corporate goals are certainly challenging, but there are a couple of more points to consider. First, as already mentioned, if marketing ROI were easy, it wouldn't be a capability that conferred the level of competitive advantage that companies such as P&G, Harrah's, and Capital One have captured. Second, each of these barriers can be and has been overcome by other marketers. In the end, it is a matter of leadership. Companies that have captured the benefits of marketing ROI invariably have leaders who created a compelling vision, achieved buy-in to a transformative and developmental roadmap, and drove organizational acceptance and compliance. The chapters that follow describe how such leaders go about this work.

Chapter 3

The Marketing ROI Mindset and Pillars

When a capability is fully developed and becomes embedded in a business, it permeates the corporate culture. A mindset evolves among the company's leaders and employees that colors the way in which they approach the world. In some cases, this mindset comes to be a primary identifying feature of the company. Six Sigma, for example, is a pervasive force within General Electric, cost control is a pervasive force within Southwest Airlines, and consumer insight is a pervasive force within Nike. Marketing ROI—optimizing marketing performance by continuously improving customer connections—can become such a force, too.

When marketing organizations properly and fully develop the marketing ROI capacity and this mindset evolves, it tends to manifest itself in five traits: a tight alignment to corporate goals, a dedicated commitment to measurement, the continuous pursuit of profitable growth, transparency in decision making and reporting, and an expanded sense of accountability.

- *A tight alignment to corporate goals.* The disconnect between marketing and the rest of the company that exists in so many businesses, and that often results in the marginalization of marketers, typically does not exist in organizations that have a marketing ROI mindset. One important reason why is that the marketers in these companies understand and align their work with the larger goals of the business. Thus, when they propose initiatives, they can demonstrate the linkage to the goals of the business at large. As a result their CEOs, CFOs, and boards are encouraged to treat them as active and credible participants in the strategic management of the enterprise.

This alignment is most commonly seen in the working relationship between marketers and finance, where the investment-versus-expense debate is most heatedly argued. GE's CMO Beth Comstock is a good example of an executive who connected her work to her company's strategic goals and bridged the breach between marketing and finance successfully. She gains the CFO's support by laying out the business case for her initiatives, setting benchmarks for interim results, and indicating her willingness to pull the plug if those benchmarks are not met. "I can't imagine doing a marketing job without connecting with the CFO," Comstock says. "Marketing must be a finance team partner."

- *A dedicated commitment to measurement.* ROI marketers are creative data collectors who are able to extract the raw information needed to fuel analytics from a variety of sources such as cost, customer attitude, and point-of-sale data. They are analytically agile—that is, skilled at using a variety of analytical tools and choosing the best tool in a given situation. And, not least of all, they are masters at convincing others to trust in the numbers, especially when those numbers contradict conventional thinking and traditional methods.

This intense commitment to measurement is another way that the marketing ROI mindset puts marketers on the same page as the CFO, the CEO, and the board. The mindset rejects the century-old myth that posits, often explicitly, that marketing is solely an art and thus, not measurable in meaningful ways. Instead, it requires that marketing be built on a foundation of fact and that the decisions of marketers be based on data and analytics.

This is not to say that measurement does not include subjective factors. ROI marketers use a wide variety of metrics that cover qualitative performance factors as well as quantitative factors, consumer attitudes as well as behaviors. Anne Finucane, Bank of America's CMO, provides a good example of how this plays out at the higher level of marketing initiatives.

"For the more general marketing efforts, the big factors we look at are sales and revenue generated by specific programs," explains Finucane. "We'll look at the overall sales. And we'll compare those numbers geographically and demographically. We have the competitive data that will produce a strong variable analysis of what it costs to make a program run successfully. From a brand perspective, we'll then examine that specific program from a couple of different views—among them, 'likelihood to recommend' and 'next-purchase consideration.' To me, those are some of the most valuable metrics we use. All together, the measurements gel. Strong brand scores along with geographic and demographic trend data, and sales and revenue numbers provide a robust report."

- *The continuous pursuit of profitable growth.* Marketers with the ROI mindset understand that revenue gains can be deceiving. Not all revenue is profitable. We got an object lesson in this reality early in our careers; we both worked at P&G and on the Citrus Hill orange juice brand at different times. In the 1980s and into the early 1990s, P&G lost money on a variable basis on every case of Citrus Hill orange juice sold. In other words, the more orange juice we sold, the more money we lost. But management was convinced that eventually "volume will allow us to fix the business." And so, Citrus Hill products were assumed to "break even" when the return on marketing spend was calculated. Of course, that fatal assumption created an even larger sinkhole as more money was spent on generating more unprofitable volume. Citrus Hill never did break even, and in late 1992, after much hard work and hundreds of millions of dollars, P&G announced it would discontinue the brand.

ROI marketers are equipped to avoid these kinds of brand debacles because their overarching objective is to deliver profitable volume. They also ensure that the measurements they gather are based in reality and utilized to improve results. Thus, they are constantly experimenting to test their hypotheses, measuring their results, and adjusting their vehicles and events in order to achieve more profitable sales.

As Rob Malcolm, the president of global marketing, sales, and innovation at Diageo PLC, says: "Marketing can't be an isolated fluffy function that does lots of creative and mysterious stuff. First and foremost, we are businesspeople who are accountable for increasing shareholder return and shareholder wealth. The growth that we drive has to be financially grounded—it must be profitable. When we talk about results and targets, we look for top-line growth in the range of 5 to 7 percent, and double-digit, bottom-line growth. Our marketers know that; they understand that. That's embedded in our culture. Profitable growth is the basic thrust of everything that we do as marketers."

- *Transparency in decision making and reporting.* The fourth trait that is common among marketers with well-developed ROI mindsets is their willingness to communicate the rationales behind their decisions and openly discuss their results.

Because their decisions are fact based, these marketers are able to easily and clearly explain them. Because they had a clear business rationale in the first place, they also don't have to hide negative results. When an experiment does not work as expected, a scientist does not hide. Instead, she learns and rethinks the hypothesis or constructs a new experiment that is more likely to prove it. This is the scientific method. ROI marketers use the same process to enhance both their performance and credibility.

At American Express Company, CMO John Hayes is identifying and communicating the metrics that will "prove" his results both before and after he invests in new marketing initiatives. "I find that my colleagues will support me," he says, "if they see the results of our successes and they also see the discipline of our efforts and, quite frankly, the transparency of our failures."

- *An expanded sense of accountability.* The final trait that ROI marketers share is their willingness to assume accountability for their results. This trait enhances the credibility of these marketers still further and encourages others to lend them their support. The ROI marketer's sense of accountability also extends beyond short-term performance to the long-term goals of both the marketing function and the enterprise at large.

Cammie Dunaway focused on this expanded sense of accountability when, in 2003, she took on the job of CMO at Yahoo!, where measurement was already a primary element of the corporate mindset. "In some ways, our business is more metrics focused and more accountable than what I saw in packaged goods," explains Dunaway (now Nintendo's executive vice president of sales and marketing). "The data that you get from online programs is so rich and is so real time that your ability to measure ROI is incredible. On the other hand, when I first came to Yahoo! I realized how easy it is to lose the forest for the trees. I saw people being very accountable for the return on a specific piece of e-mail, for example, but not as knowledgeable as they should have been about how that effort contributed to the overall health of our business."

Like any true and fully evolved mindset, the ROI marketing mindset can spread throughout a corporate culture. It can, in fact, become a primary driver of an entire company's performance and success and have a dramatic impact far beyond its point of origination. To illustrate what that impact might look like and how it is developed, consider the story of Capital One Financial Corp.

CAPITAL ONE REINVENTS THE CREDIT CARD BUSINESS

Capital One is best known as one of the nation's leading credit card issuers and the company whose ads featured barbarian hordes invading suburban neighborhoods with the tagline "What's in *your* wallet?" In 2006, after completing the $14.6 billion acquisition of North Fork Bancorporation, it also became one of the 10 largest U.S. banks. That year, Capital One's revenues exceeded $15 billion, and it boasted almost 50 million customer accounts. The company has come a long way in a short time on the coattails of a single idea.

Rich Fairbank and Nigel Morris, two consultants retained to turn around the unprofitable operations of a major bank, got that idea in the mid-1980s. As they reviewed the institution's credit card business, an epiphany struck: credit cards are not banking, they're information. "It's all about collecting information on 200 million people that you'd never meet, and on the basis of that information, making a series of very critical long term decisions about lending money to them and hoping they would pay you back," Fairbank later said.[1]

Fairbank and Morris became convinced that customer data and sophisticated analytics could be blended to tailor products that would meet the needs of different types of customers. After all, millionaires probably used their cards differently than striving young families did; some customers paid off their balance religiously every month while others rolled it over at 20 percent interest. The questions were: who was doing what and why? and, how could that information be used to create more appealing—and profitable—offerings?

The problem was that all of the potentially lucrative information needed was sitting in the company's banking clients' IT system like a load of bricks dumped on the sidewalk. There were no plans to build anything useful out of the data; no one even knew how to mix the mortar that could hold it all together. Nevertheless, the consultants convinced the bank to run some tests based on rudimentary statistical techniques. A random set of consumers got offers for credit cards at one interest rate; another group received a different proposition entirely. The results were measured and showed promise, but the idea of creating different offers for different customers proved to be too out-of-the-box for their client. Rather than doing more of what worked, as the two consultants advised, the bank jettisoned the program.

This did not deter Fairbank and Morris. They had become zealots for the cause of microsegmentation and mass customization based on the scientific principle of testing hypotheses and measuring and building on positive results. Their zealotry was based, Morris said, on "a tremendous passion for doing things right and doing them based on facts."[2] All they needed was a bank where they could put their passion to good use. Such an institution was not easy to find in an industry that traditionally depended more on the credit decisions of seasoned executives than on the rigorous analysis of the reams of data it generated.

After more than 20 rejections—with responses ranging from rabidly hostile to frustratingly indifferent—Signet Banking, based in Richmond, Virginia, bought into the consultants' vision. It had one condition, however. Fairbank and Morris had to join the firm. The partners countered with their own demand: they wanted complete control, not only over the credit card division's strategy but also over its marketing and IT operations. "We warned them that this would require virtually starting over, rebuilding a very different company," Fairbank said. "We had to create a culture that was very nonhierarchical and challenged everything."[3]

This meant reengineering processes; empowering employees with information, tools, and responsibility and holding them accountable for their decisions; creating a culture where decisions would be based on rigorous analysis and testing rather than gut feelings and guesswork; and most of all, ensuring that marketing spend would become a fact-based investment yielding high returns instead of a money-losing exercise in creative tub thumping. Although Fairbank and Morris might not describe what they did in the same terms, we would say that they created an environment in which the marketing ROI mindset could flourish.

This was a daunting task in 1988. For example, the records of millions of transactions that could have provided insight into how Signet's customers used their credit were being systematically erased so that the $40 computer tapes could be recycled. But the erstwhile consultants rolled up their sleeves and began to execute the theories they had developed as outsiders looking in. They were so confident of delivering a hefty return on investment, in fact, that they tied their own compensation to a percentage of the value of the new accounts they would deliver to Signet.

They got off to a wobbly start, launching products using a combination of Signet's traditional credit algorithms and shrink-wrapped modeling software. "The results were disastrous," reported a Harvard Business School case study on the company. "Signet's charge-off rate rose from 2 percent, among the industry's best, to more than 6 percent, among the industry's worst."[4]

But Fairbank and Morris persisted. More to the point, they tested ... and tested and tested. "Testing is a way for the best ideas to rise to the top," Fairbank said. "We're not just taking huge amounts of information; we're creating a massive scientific lab."[5] In a multistep process, they would first build a business case and find a target market for a new offer. Then, they would vary the offer, switching around elements to see which combinations worked and which didn't. Then, they would micro-segment by sending pitches to different demographic and psychographic clusters, again refining the offers and broadening the tests as the results came in.

Then in 1991 the company rolled out a breakthrough offer that doubled its business within a year and changed the face of the industry. It offered selected consumers low introductory interest rates if they would transfer their outstanding balances on competitor's cards to a Signet credit card. Interestingly, by the time the competition caught up with their concept, Fairbank and Morris already had moved on to other innovative offers. Their analysis showed that the teaser rates were attracting too many unprofitable customers.

Fairbank and Morris's successes caused Signet's managed credit card portfolio to swell from just over $1 billion in 1988 to almost $6.5 billion in 1994. With its credit card division generating about two-thirds of the bank's revenues, from 1992 until 1994, Signet was the best-performing stock on the New York Stock Exchange. In October 1994, the bank cashed in, spinning off its credit card business in a $1.1 billion initial public offering (IPO). Fairbank was named chairman and CEO of Capital One Financial Corp.; Morris became president and COO.

Of course, Fairbank and Morris's run was just beginning. Their conviction that the key to profitable marketing was transforming data into action has evolved into a formal test-and-learn philosophy that Capital One calls its Information Based Strategy (IBS). IBS is powered in part by the hundreds of thousands of offers the company has tested over the years. The collected results of these tests have evolved into highly sophisticated predictive models. These models enable the company to match microsegments of consumers (often overlooked by its competitors) to offerings that have been tailored specifically to the consumers' behaviors and other critical variables. The rewards of this ability have been substantial indeed: Capital One's earnings-per-share (EPS) growth rate has averaged 29 percent annually since its IPO, and it has ascended to 154th slot on the Fortune 500 rankings.

THE ELEMENTS OF CAPITAL ONE'S SUCCESS

We have been describing a mindset—a cultural orientation within a function that can, in certain environments and with the proper encouragement, spread throughout business when the capacity for marketing ROI is fully developed. But what are the primary elements of this capacity? And how is it developed? The answers to these two questions are revealed by delving a little deeper into how Capital One operates.

One key element can be found in Capital One's rigorously analytical approach to understanding which of its marketing offers generates the most profitable return on investment. In fact, each of its offers is a test, one of thousands of informed questions in search of working hypotheses. Do cat lovers carry larger balances than dog lovers do? Which group defaults more frequently? Who will pay an annual fee? How much will they pay? What should they get in return? Do they prefer a fixed or variable interest rate? At Capital One, the answers to these questions are written in spreadsheets, not stone, and results are continually retested. The company uses analytics to determine what works and what does not. Without some kind of analytical rigor, Capital One would be forced to either mindlessly replicate what it had done in the past (which is exactly what all of its competitors were doing back in 1994) or take random shots in the dark.

Another element we see in place at Capital One is a set of decision support tools that routinize the analytics, making them consistent, comprehensive, and comprehensible to the company's employees. Customized software at Capital One's call centers, for example, recognizes a customer's phone number and characterizes that individual according to 12 criteria (e.g., what Capital One products he or she currently uses; past responsiveness to new offers). Tools like this one have enabled Capital One to decentralize its decision making and push it out to employees at the point of customer contact. The company uses similar analysis and decision support tools throughout its business, even in its human resources process, in which predictive models built on the performance of its current employees are used to identify the most promising job candidates.

Yet another element that contributes to Capital One's ROI mindset can be seen in its business processes—in how the company routinizes its operations. The software that the company's service associates use is embedded in a process. Once a customer is recognized, the call is routed to one of 7,000 associates who, based on criteria such as training and availability, is most likely to be of assistance. Since there are literally thousands of possible offers, each associate can only be expected to be familiar with a finite number. When a customer call arrives, a menu of likely cross-selling opportunities, all of which the associate is thoroughly familiar with, pops up on his or her screen. From day one, Capital One has been building processes that ensure the integration and the full utilization of all of the company's analytical prowess and decision support tools. The outputs of these processes are fact-based decisions (many of which can now be made by customer-facing staff), the refinement of offers, and profitable growth.

The final element that contributes to the ROI mindset at Capital One is perhaps the least mentioned: the organization-wide alignment—the support and motivation—that ensures that its processes are executed. This high degree of organizational alignment and support is clearly based in the fact that the company was founded on data, analytics, and the ability to put them to work to produce profits. In this sense, Capital One's mindset is a genetic trait, inherited from Fairbank and Morris. This alignment and support can be found in the fact that there are no barriers between the business analysis, market research, statistics, management information systems (MISs), brand marketing and financial accounting functions. This degree of alignment, Morris told *American Banker*, "requires commitment from senior management that is nothing short of totally resolute."[6] Capital One also trains its employees to succeed, fosters innovative thinking, and ties incentives to achievement. It seeks out entrepreneurial personalities who will thrive in an atmosphere of constant change. It interviews and tests their skills rigorously, then provides extensive training and promotion opportunities after they are hired. Each employee's compensation is based on a customized plan that's tied to sales, productivity, and quality of service based on ratings not only from superiors but also from peers and direct reports. A corporate success story like Capital One, which, by the way, is also on *Fortune* magazine's 100 Best Places to Work list, is the result of an entire organization that is fully aligned and working toward common goals.

To summarize, it is the development and integration of these four elements—analytics, decision support tools, processes, and organizational alignment—that set the stage of Capital One's success and gave rise to the mindset that continues to have such a pervasive effect on how the company approaches its markets. Of course, Capital One is a unique example of the power of the ROI mindset in that Fairbank and Morris had Signet's entire credit card business and eventually, after the IPO, the entire company at their command. That is not to say, however, that marketing executives cannot use the same underlying methodology to produce a functional transformation or that what starts in marketing cannot spread beyond its borders. They can, and it can.

THE FOUR PILLARS OF THE MARKETING ROI CAPABILITY

The same four elements that were integrated at Capital One to produce its mindset are also the basic building blocks—the pillars—of the marketing ROI mindset. Here are the four pillars:

- *Analytics.* These enable marketers to collect data regarding the outcomes of its events and analyze that data to understand why those outcomes were produced.
- *Decision support tools.* These tools empower marketers by converting their analytical findings into routinized knowledge that is distributed throughout the organization and applied to improve the results of current and future events.
- *Process.* This element ensures the full integration and utilization of analytics and decision support in the planning, execution, and measurement of events.
- *Organizational alignment.* This pillar delivers the support, such as centers of excellence, and creates the motivation, such as incentives, that marketers need to staff and carry out the processes.

PILLAR ONE: ANALYTICS

The marketing ROI capability runs on an analytical engine, and the fuel this engine consumes is data. Analytics enable a precise understanding of the incremental volumes and sales that different events generate. When the engine is firing on all cylinders, it is capable of clearly identifying profitable events and helping marketers avoid unwittingly planning events that produce negative returns.

Beyond the fact that analytics are a complex mathematical science outside the experience of most marketers, there are several other issues that make analytics a difficult pillar to erect. For one, there is a large and ever-growing selection of analytical tools being offered to marketers. But evaluating their efficacy and choosing the right ones is a challenge that many marketers are not prepared to undertake. Second, analytics are only as good as the data that fuels them. The *right* data sources must be identified and captured, a task that always requires thoughtful rigor, but which in industries, such as the automotive sector, where consumer data has not been systematically collected in the past, can sometimes be highly problematic.

In the next chapter, we will explore analytics and reach out for the simplicity and clarity that is needed to build awareness on a day-to-day basis. We will describe how to impose some order on the many available analytics and identify a set of them that is aligned to your internal capabilities, industry, and data availability. We will also address the data conundrum—what kinds you need and where to find them.

PILLAR TWO: DECISION SUPPORT TOOLS

The decision support tools of the second pillar are the user-friendly interface between complex analytical output and marketers who often are scattered throughout the enterprise. These tools collect, integrate, and apply data from the analytical engine and from the field in support of marketing activities such as planning advertising and promotion events, measuring results against plans, and so on.

This second pillar enables you to automate the application of analytical knowledge, expanding its availability and ensuring its rigorous use throughout the marketing organization. It provides marketers with a level of insight into the profitability of their events that they have never before enjoyed. In doing so, it drives sound decision-making closer to the customer, creates the flexibility needed to capture optimal results on the frontlines, and enhances application discipline.

In Chapter 5, we explore the considerations specific to the decision support tools pillar: how to choose tools, and whether and how to bundle them to enhance ease of use and effectiveness; the need to update them to keep their output fresh and relevant; and the execution issues that can reduce their effectiveness and cause them to mislead marketers.

PILLAR THREE: PROCESSES

The third pillar integrates analytics and decision support tools with the strategic and operational activities that comprise the marketing ROI loop (described in the previous chapter). These processes, which occur within the "hub" of the loop, are the glue that holds the capability together. They ensure that marketing activities are properly executed, as well as coordinated, embedded, and capable of producing the optimal profit, volume, and spending targets event by event, account by account, geography by geography.

The third pillar imposes order on marketing through four processes, as shown in Exhibit 3-1:

- *Target setting*, which enables marketers to set realistic goals, define the right set of metrics for measuring them, and cascade those goals down to the proper levels of the organization
- *Planning*, which defines the offers, vehicles, allocation of resources over time, geographies and events, and then, predicts expected outcomes

83

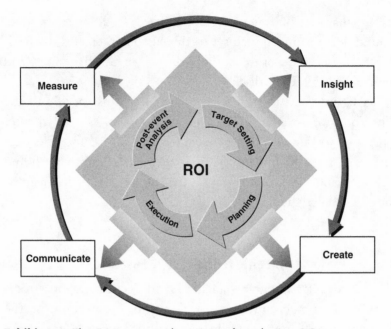

Exhibit 3-1 The Processes at the Heart of Marketing ROI

- *Execution,* which ensures that events happen as planned and creates the flexibility to respond quickly to changing circumstances
- *Post-event analysis,* which measures results, surfaces the root causes of the differences between expected and actual outcomes, and captures the lessons that will improve outcomes in the future.

In Chapter 6, we describe how these processes, which already exist in truncated forms in many marketing organizations, can be redesigned to incorporate rigorous performance standards and to support a test-and-learn mindset. We also explore how these processes can be integrated to close the loop and enhance the credibility, accountability, and success of ROI marketers.

PILLAR FOUR: ORGANIZATIONAL ALIGNMENT

The final pillar ensures that the organizational support and motivation needed to develop and maintain the marketing ROI capability is forthcoming. Without this pillar, which too often is overlooked, it is impossible to meet the challenges inherent in fundamental changes, such as decentralizing tactical, knowledge-based decision making and deploying a redesigned marketing strategy that properly balances volume and profit objectives. The organizational issues addressed in this pillar include the support needed to establish the capability, the definition of roles and responsibilities of the people who will make sure the processes are executed, and the creation and alignment of the incentives required to motivate everyone involved in those processes.

In Chapter 7, we explore a host of considerations around organizational alignment. We discuss the need to develop support not only within marketing but also from senior leadership, across functions, and sometimes beyond the boundaries of the company itself. We will describe the considerations around the establishment of clear decision rights and the training and empowerment of executives and staff, as well as the development of the center of excellence that will provide the analytical fire-power on which marketing ROI depends. Finally, we will examine the considerations around incentives, including the need to align them as closely as possible to profitable growth in both a local and a corporate sense.

Every marketing organization that undertakes the challenge of building a capability around marketing ROI must develop these four pillars. They will have their own data and their own customer dynamics and targets. In other words, the exact mechanics and complexity will be unique in each case. But at the structural level, each will have these four pillars and their associated subcomponents.

THE INTEGRATION IMPERATIVE

Before we move ahead to the next four chapters and explore each of the pillars in greater depth, it is important to understand that the four pillars of marketing ROI are *load-bearing*, an engineering term that refers to an element that cannot be left out or removed without compromising the stability and integrity of the whole. None of the pillars and no combination of them that does not include all four can support the capability and mindset on their own. As seen in Exhibit 3-2, they stand together to create and support an integrated effort.

This becomes obvious when you consider the irreplaceable nature of each pillar and how they work together to support the

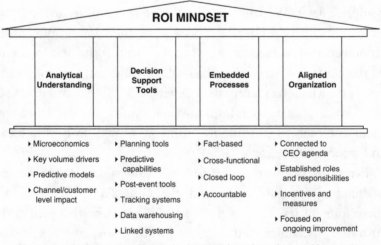

Exhibit 3-2 The Four Pillars of Marketing ROI

marketing ROI capability: Marketers must have analytics to measure events. But the analytics are too complex and time-consuming for people to repeatedly calculate; marketers need systems and tools to turn the information into practical knowledge. They also need to have a process to make sure this happens and that the knowledge is applied. And, finally, marketers must have the organizational support and incentives to make sure that people want to make the wheel turn.

As logical and obvious as this may sound, far too many would-be ROI marketers are tripped up by this imperative. One reason this happens is because many companies already have portions of the pillars in place. Every marketing department has a planning process in place. Many companies have purchased analytics that measure marketing ROI on an ad hoc basis, from one-off studies to spreadsheets to more sophisticated solutions that are not widely applied. But ad hoc analytics are localized solutions; they simply can't develop the horsepower required to pull a company, its employees, and marketing into a closed loop that continuously improves customer connections and drives profitable growth.

Sometimes marketers have great organizations with skilled people and newly reengineered processes, but they don't have any analytic capability and thus have no predictive capability. Sometimes they have great analytical engines, but their tools and systems are so cumbersome that their marketers and salespeople simply will not use them. The reality is that few enterprises have all of the necessary components of marketing ROI working together, aimed in the right direction, and delivering its full potential.

Another reason why the marketing function is not integrated is that companies tend to try to solve marketing problems that require fundamental change with simple and easy-to-implement "silver bullets." They act as if it's a problem of analytics (hence the quest for ever-better modeling tools) or systems (thus the growth of the customer relationship management [CRM] industry); or it can be solved by better processes (we can fix it at an offsite meeting!) or organizational changes (such as getting sales and marketing to cooperate *once and for all*). This capability, however, requires that improvements in the effectiveness of marketing be all-encompassing and systemic in nature.

Perhaps the most common integration mistake occurs when marketers fall for the black box myth. The promise and the potential of analytics and decision support tools captivate them. These sophisticated IT tools *can* produce amazingly accurate predictions and provide a "front end" that makes manipulating those predictions both easy and intuitive. There are many companies that use analytics to predict the outcomes of marketing programs with 98 percent accuracy. The problem is that the black box is so enticing that sometimes marketers buy it and forget all about its context. It requires consistent data streams, a process to guide the timing of outputs, a robust post-event analysis, and a host of other capabilities that are inherent in the other pillars to produce outcomes that are that accurate and ensure that the capability is institutionalized. If those capabilities aren't forthcoming, the box stops working.

Finally, the integration of the four pillars into a single capability often fails because companies simply don't want to face the hard work involved in one or more of the pillars. So, for example, they will skip the organizational alignment pillar because changing their organization's culture is so painful and time consuming. They try to gain a partial benefit by building the pillars that they can mostly easily influence, but they avoid those that entail political risk. This approach will not work; marketing ROI initiatives can be scaled to any size, but as stated above, each of the pillars must be in place.

So, the bad news is that the integration imperative can be an elusive demand. When pillars are missing or not fully developed, the structure on which the capability depends collapses. Marketing profitability becomes a pipe dream. But, the good news is if you develop each of the four pillars completely, they will, by definition, be integrated. What is the twofold secret to mastering the integration challenge? Don't be fooled about where you are in the journey, and don't stop short of your final destination.

Chapter 4

Building Analytical Prowess

The goal of marketing ROI is to invest the *right* amount of money in marketing activities in the *right* way across brands, geographies, and vehicles in order to bolster connections with customers and the profitability of customer relationships. To attain that goal, marketers must be able to measure event results, identify the causes of those results, and use that knowledge to predict the outcomes of future events. The measurement and forecasting of results requires data and a set of analytical approaches. These are the primary components of the analytics pillar, the first pillar of marketing ROI capability.

The marketer's need to develop analytical prowess—the ability to utilize data and analytical approaches to optimize the return on marketing spend—is already well established. For some time, senior marketers have been questioning the conventional ROI assumptions of the past. As Rob Malcolm, Diageo's senior marketing executive, says: "It's easy to start with a presumption that because we're comfortable with TV, we don't have to question its effectiveness: 'We'll continue to use it because we're used to it.'"[1]

Further, top marketers are demanding that ROI rigor be employed across their marketing spend. "We also applied hard metrics to our sponsorships," Jerri DeVard, the former CMO of Verizon, explains. "People came to us and said, 'There are going to be a million people at this event, and you can hang your sign over there.' We made them tell us how we were going to generate sales, and we looked for an ROI of about four to one—because we're all living in a world of aggressive goals and limited dollars."[2]

There is a widespread recognition among marketers across the corporate spectrum that analytical competence is a prerequisite of marketing success. In fact, as seen in Exhibit 4-1, Booz & Company surveys with the Association of National Advertisers (ANA) revealed that ROI analytics and consumer insights (many of which are derived from analytics) are the two capabilities that marketers identify as the most important that they can develop.[3]

For all of the interest in analytics, however, relatively few marketers have mastered the intricacies of this pillar. Based on our interactions with senior marketing executives, only one in twenty of them has fully developed analytical prowess. How then can you inject some clarity into the situation and begin erecting the first pillar of marketing ROI?

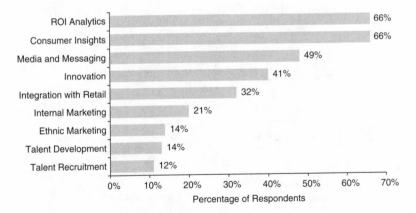

Source: ANA/Booz & Company Analysis

Exhibit 4-1 New Capabilities That Marketing Requires

IMPOSING ORDER ON DATA

In 2005, an ANA task force studied best practices in marketing accountability. As the task force surveyed marketing accountability across industries, it noted, "The key driver of difference among verticals is the availability of reliable, granular, malleable and relevant data."[4] Information-rich data supports accountability because it is the raw material used in the establishment of baselines for setting targets and measuring results. For this same reason, high-quality data is also the key driver in the development of the first pillar of marketing ROI.

Data is the fuel that analytical engines consume. Various types of data are needed to run marketing analytics. Constructing the analytics pillar requires that marketers understand how to identify and collect these different kinds of data.

A logical way to impose some order on the issue of data is to relate it to the ROI formula introduced in Chapter 2, as shown in Exhibit 4-2. Determining the ROI of an event requires three subcalculations: total spend, variable contribution margin (VCM), and incremental volume. There are two broad categories of data

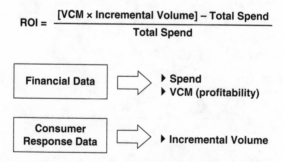

$$ROI = \frac{[VCM \times Incremental\ Volume] - Total\ Spend}{Total\ Spend}$$

Financial Data ⇒ ▸ Spend
▸ VCM (profitability)

Consumer Response Data ⇒ ▸ Incremental Volume

Exhibit 4-2 Two Data Types That Drive ROI Calculation

needed to calculate these values: financial data, which includes data pertaining to event costs and product/service profitability; and consumer response data, which includes data pertaining to purchase transactions and consumer attitudes.

Financial Data

For the purposes of marketing ROI, financial data comes in two varieties. The first is data pertaining to the cost of the event. This data, as you may have already realized, determines the "total spend" component of the ROI formula. Event cost data includes all of the expenses incurred preparing for, staging, and responding to an event. For a golf tournament sponsorship, for example, that might include the sponsorship fee; the cost of designing, printing, and installing signage; and the ancillary costs of hosting guests, such as tent rental, catering, and waitstaff. For an online banner ad that might include the cost of design, placement fee, cost per click, and any expenses related to monitoring the ad's performance and responses.

It is relatively easy to collect event cost data. Typically, these expenses are paid from the marketing budget and are approved within the function, so marketers have direct access to them. Complications can arise, however, when individual events are part of a larger program or media buys are outsourced. In cases like these, event costs often are bundled and isolating the data at the individual event level may require a little extra work on the marketer's or the vendor's part. Highly decentralized marketing spend, common in retail banking and with some retailers, can create another barrier to collecting event cost data. This may require creating data collection processes that extend throughout the organization.

The second type of financial data required to power ROI analytics is product or service profitability data. This is the data that is used to determine the VCM component of the ROI formula. As explained in Chapter 2, profitability data includes much of the information that companies use to calculate their margins such as the selling price, variable cost of goods sold, and other variable costs like shipping. (It does not include fixed costs such as overhead in a plant or at headquarters.) Essentially, this data answers the question, "How much money do we make when we sell an extra widget due to our marketing program?"

Profitability data is essential to the calculation of marketing ROI, but it can be more difficult for marketers to collect. Marketers' access to such data varies widely. Some companies embrace the concept of "open-book management" and share profitability data across the organization; others, including at least one major bank, refuse to provide even their senior marketers with profitability data. This latter condition never ceases to amaze us. How can employees be expected to pursue profit if they aren't allowed to examine the financial results of their work? Additional complications also arise in the calculation of VCM because it is a measure that many finance departments do not currently use and because some companies group their expenses into line items that make it difficult to isolate variable costs from fixed costs. In other cases, some companies don't account for costs with enough precision to enable reasonably efficient data collection. The result is that collecting profitability data can require changes in the reporting system. Nevertheless, there is a silver lining: profitability data is internal data, and when marketers make a strong business case for gaining access to it and enlist the support of their colleagues in finance, they usually not only are able to obtain it but also, in doing so, have an opportunity to begin creating organizational buy-in to the ROI mindset.

Customer Response Data

Customer response data determines the "incremental volume" component of the ROI formula. It also comes in two varieties. The first, with which marketers will be most familiar, is self-reported data, that is, information that customers provide about themselves. Self-reported data includes attitudinal data such as brand loyalty, awareness, and willingness to recommend as well as purchase data (in this case, information that customers volunteer about their purchases).

Self-reported data encompasses many measures, but it is relatively easy to collect. Most large companies have in-house market research departments that collect data by surveying current and potential customers to learn about their attitudes and behaviors vis-à-vis the company's brands. There are also many external sources of this data, which is gathered by independent research firms that package and sell it and/or accept commissions for dedicated studies.

There are several issues to consider when using self-reported data. For one, people do not always report their own attitudes and behavior with full fidelity. They may say they intend to buy when they don't, or that they purchased x amount of product over a specific time period when they didn't. Another issue is the rigor and consistency with which self-reported data is gathered. For instance, over time, survey questions are often changed, which makes it difficult to maintain baselines and compare results.

The second variety of customer response data is behavioral data. This can be data regarding behavior observed or recorded, such as test drives at car dealerships or forwarding an e-mail to a friend. But most often, it is transactional data. Transactional data is collected at the point of purchase from scanners at cash registers; from retailers, dealers, and distributors; and from a variety of other sources. It tells the marketer what the customer bought, where and at what time the purchase was made, the frequency of repurchase, and other hard facts. Transactional data is the most valuable ROI data because it represents actual customer behavior and is not dependent on customers' memories or their inclination to tell the truth. Thus, transactional data reveals the customer's buying response and provides the most solid foundation for an accurate calculation of incremental volume.

ROI marketers seek transactional data at the lowest level possible in order to better tease out the incremental volume produced by their events. For example, they prefer to collect data at the store or dealer level rather than the regional level; they go to the household level rather than city level. The lower the level at which the data is collected, the higher the variation and the better the analytical output. The minimum level at which they seek data is the level at which marketing event investments will be made. If they run a TV ad at the city level, then they seek city-level purchase data. If they run a print ad on the East Coast, then they need East Coast–level purchase data.

Transactional data can be the hardest for marketers to obtain. Often, it is not readily available. Recently, a marketer at a designer apparel manufacturer, who wanted to determine the ROI of the company's annual Fashion Week advertising blitz, encountered this barrier. He was able to capture transactional data from the company-owned stores, but the department stores that sell the majority of his company's apparel refused to share their transaction data because they viewed the company-owned stores as direct competitors. (In this case, his only option was to model the advertising impact in the company stores and extrapolate that impact to the larger universe of department stores.)

Just as often, marketers simply are not aware of the data that is available to them. Marketers from pharmaceutical companies invariably say that they cannot obtain the same level of detailed response data that CPG marketers enjoy. But every filled prescription is recorded, and firms such as IMS Health, which gathers information from 850 million prescription sales in 100 countries each month, have created huge repositories of this data.[5] Pharmaceutical marketers are well aware of these databases; in fact, many of them already buy aggregated data and analytics from IMS. So when these marketers say they can't get the data, it is often a reflexive answer. They simply have not thought about how to obtain response data at the granular level and best use it.

The same reflexive statements are commonly heard regarding many of today's emerging-marketing vehicles such as mobile ad campaigns and social utilities. Again, marketers say that they cannot get the response data required to tease out incremental volume. And again, the real problem is that they have not thought the data challenge through. The data exists, but marketers have not yet identified what information they need, whether it is worth getting (why gather data to optimize ROI on a vehicle that accounts for a very small portion of your spend?), and how to get it.

THREE QUESTIONS ABOUT DATA

Some marketers are awash in a sea of data, especially those who engage customers through digital media. For instance, Yahoo's former CMO, Cammie Dunaway, recently said about the online media giant, "We collect a Library of Congress's worth of information every day, and we're very committed to the power of data." Others are data starved, such as the bank marketing executive who was not allowed access to the profitability data for the products and services she was charged with selling. No matter what your condition, the best way to approach the data challenge is to ask the following three questions.

Question #1: What Data Do You Already Have?

List the financial and customer response data that is currently available to you by marketing vehicle, and organize it into the classifications described above. Track each data stream back to its source, and determine the lowest level at which it is collected. Also, identify those sources that yield the most plentiful data. As we've said, the best data is closest to the point of purchase, and the more data points you can collect, the more variation your analytical results will have and the more robust they will be.

Question #2: If the Available Data Isn't Sufficient, Where Can You Go to Get More?

Identify the data gaps, whether they are in event cost, profitability, self-reported, or transactional data. Then, ask yourself how and where that data is collected and how you can induce the owner of the data to share it with you.

Financial Data

For event cost, you can turn to your vendors for help. Keeping your business should be incentive enough for vendors to start the flow of event-level data. For example, you may ask your media buyer who buys for television to begin reporting spending and Gross Ratings Points (GRPs) by major cities or geographic regions. The field marketing and sales organizations are another, often untapped source of event data, particularly when they are responsible for the spending at bar and sports promotions and sampling events. Whenever a company's employees are spending on events, they should be reporting event-level cost data; better yet, event cost reporting should be built into their work process. (We discuss this topic in greater detail in Chapter 6.)

For profitability data, call on the finance department. The quest to measure and improve ROI should resonate there. Access to accurate profitability data is also one of the reasons why the best CMOs have established strong working relationships with CFOs.

Customer Response Data

For self-reported data, call on your company's market researchers or seek out external market research firms. If, as for so many marketers, a gap exists in the transactional data, consider the potential sources of this data. If your company sells directly to consumers or other end users of your products, transactional data should be available, even if it may require some effort to obtain. If you don't have direct access to the sales transactions, identify the point of purchase and the owner of the data produced there. Ask yourself how to gain access to the data stream. And don't forget to consider credit and loyalty card data.

In some cases, such as the marketer at the fashion apparel manufacturer who couldn't get transaction data from department stores, incentives could be an effective means of gaining access.

Perhaps one of the conditions attached to the manufacturer's co-op advertising dollars could be access to retailer's transactional data. In other cases, you might consider buying the data directly from its owners. R.J. Reynolds Tobacco Company did this in the 1990s when it wanted transactional data on cigarette sales in convenience stores. (The reporting system the company built with IRI—Information Resources, Inc.—eventually became the standard transactional data source for the entire industry.) In still other cases, you might purchase the data from third parties such as J.D. Power and Associates and ACNielsen.

Question #3: What Can You Determine from the Data?

Data dictates an analytical approach, and different analytics provide different information regarding the outcomes of marketing events and how they can be optimized. In order to answer this last question, we need to turn from data to analytics.

DEMYSTIFYING ANALYTICS

There is no "silver bullet" in ROI analytics, that is, no single analytic approach that is always the best choice to meet the various constraints that marketers face in the real and often chaotic world of business. In actuality, the data that marketers collect can be utilized in several different types of analytics. Some analytics produce more accurate results than others. Some are more mathematically sophisticated than others. But, when properly utilized, all of them can produce viable answers for ROI marketers. Thus, these marketers understand their analytical options and how to choose among them.

There are three broad categories of analytic approaches: behavior analytics, attitudinal analytics, and business case analytics.

Behavioral Analytics

Behavioral marketing analytics are driven by models, which, in turn, are driven by algorithms and fueled by transactional data. These analytics predict how customers will respond as marketers run events such as a price change, a promotion, or a TV ad. Theoretically, as long as the necessary data is available, models can be constructed to predict any kind of customer behavior. But in practice, the most valuable models are those that predict the purchase behavior of customers.

The ACNielsen Company, the marketing research firm that built its reputation tracking consumer goods and, later, television viewers, was a pioneer in the field of marketing models, and it continues those efforts today in new media. When John Porter, a young statistician fresh out of graduate school, arrived at Nielsen almost 30 years ago, the company's auditors were still checking the inventory of more than 2,000 grocery stores by sight, deducting their tallies from hardcopy purchasing records, and issuing sales figures on a bimonthly basis. Porter took on the assignment of improving the accuracy of Nielsen's processes.

The data Nielsen was collecting was suitable for tracking long-term trends such as year-to-year comparisons, because there was little variation. "It was exactly the right thing for strategic decision making," Porter says, "but it didn't have the tactical richness you need to build models."[6] The rich data streams needed for more accurate models began to trickle out starting in 1974, when a device built by the National Cash Register Co. scanned a 10-pack of Wrigley's Juicy Fruit gum at a supermarket in Troy, Ohio. The bar code and scanner era had dawned and within five years, Nielsen's SCANTRACK service was providing clients with customized reports on market trends based on the bar code data collected by scanners in several markets.

At first, these new data streams were frustrating to Porter and his boss, Bill Hawkes. Previously, when they were looking at sales data over a two-month period, the patterns had been relatively smooth and straightforward. But now, when they looked at weekly scanner data, they saw what resembled a geological survey of the Alps, replete with towering peaks and plunging valleys. Nobody would trust numbers that seemed to bounce so erratically, they thought. So, Hawkes and Porter figured out how to smooth out the highs and lows so the weekly numbers looked more like the bimonthly figures that came out of the physical audits. They even went so far as to present a paper, "The Advances and Practice of Marketing Science," at an industry conference in 1983, that showed how to make all those nasty discrepancies disappear. Then, about a month after the conference, the pair were mulling over the data yet again and suddenly felt "really stupid." The bounces were not so erratic after all. They were caused by trade promotions—in other words, by the discounts, ads, and offers that manufacturers underwrite and retailers agree to make to entice customers to buy manufacturers' products in their stores.

"We had been focusing on the wrong thing, the smooth part," Porter says. "The light came on that we ought to focus on the rough part." The pair quickly realized that they could determine whether a display or a feature ad caused a bump in sales. They could measure the impact of a price discount. The effect of seasonality on volume became as clear as a cloudless day.

Not only did the peaks and valleys indicate what had happened historically, that information could be plugged into simple regression models and the impact of different drivers on future sales could be predicted. Hawkes and Porter had cracked the code on the impact of pricing and promotion on sales volume.

That same year, Porter and Hawkes made a presentation to Nielsen's management steering committee. The company was at a crossroads, they declared. If it did not get into the modeling business and start offering predictive analytics to its clients, someone else would use Nielsen's data and do it themselves—driving the company out of the advisory space that it had occupied for 50 years. To its credit, the management team decided on the spot to fund a pilot program and told Hawkes and Porter to come up with a business plan for incorporating analytical modeling into Nielsen's offerings to its clients.

Since then, ACNielsen, along with competitors such as Information Resources Inc. (IRI), Marketing Management Analytics, Inc., and Promotion Decisions, Inc., and dozens of academics and consultants have been refining marketing models. The behavior models developed over the last 25 years allow marketers to isolate the individual impacts of factors such as advertising, pricing, promotion, word of mouth, special events, and seasonality, as well as variables that they have little or no control over such as weather or competitive response on volume and ROI. They utilize multivariate regression analysis to manipulate data around a series of variables and produce a simple and often highly accurate prediction.

New marketing models designed to help companies manage and optimize their spending in new media are also emerging. For instance, Yahoo Consumer Direct teamed up with ACNielsen to offer marketers a program that allows them not only to reach very specific customer segments online but also to measure the responses of the customers based on the tracking of actual purchases. In its "Most Valuable Consumer" program, marketers purchase access to specific, sharply focused customer segments from Yahoo, which distributes the marketers' banner ads or promotions to these customers throughout its massive online network. Then, ACNielsen enters the picture. It uses its market research prowess to create a statistically significant panel of tens of thousands of people within the customer segment, calculates the offline sales impact of the ads or promotions within the panel, and extrapolates those results over the entire customer segment, which often ranges into the millions of people. The result is an ROI figure that is accurate enough that marketers can use it to predict and improve the results of their online events.

When you only focus on a model's output—the prediction or the actual result, it's easy to see how they get mistaken for black boxes. But they aren't. As you've already read, building effective models requires specialized statistical skills and marketing expertise to create a robust algorithm and choose the right data streams.

Today, several analytics companies are busy building and refining the "holy grail" of marketing analytics—the modeling of a company's entire marketing mix. Marketing mix models can tell you how much of your brand spending to invest in various vehicles such as print, TV, radio, and Internet. San Mateo, California–based M-Factor, for example, has built a model that can cover all marketing vehicles and turned it into a software-based service it calls "M3," which is being used by major marketers as Coca-Cola. M3's simulation analytics and monitoring diagnostics enable marketers to predict outcomes across brands, channels, and vehicles, modeling thousands of event permutations on a daily basis if they wish. The potential value of marketing mix models is enormous; according to a study by the Marketing

Leadership Council, companies expect that these models will boost returns on their marketing spend by 20 to 30 percent.[7]

MODELING A PRICE CHANGE

Models do much more than simply telling marketers how well their events worked after the fact. More importantly, they generate predictions about what will work in the future—the most valuable information marketers can obtain. In the early 2000s, a leading over-the-counter pharmaceutical company sought to predict the effects of a proposed price increase on a popular first aid ointment. A model was constructed, and data for multiple variables such as mass media, pricing, and promotion, covering a period of months before a price increase, were fed into it. It predicted that the price increase would not significantly reduce volume.

The analysis of results for three months after the price increase revealed that the higher price slightly reduced volume but that the health of the brand and several other factors contributed to an overall rise in volume. The model also revealed that an increase in annual profits could be gained if the company followed a set of guidelines:

- Holding its price in the face of increased private label competition
- Raising prices further during the ointment's "off-peak" selling seasons
- Increasing print advertising just prior to the ointment's peak selling season to create additional lift at a low cost
- Using trade promotions very cautiously, as they were unprofitable

---

Attitudinal Analytics

Attitudinal analytics measure customer opinions, perceptions, and self-reported behaviors. Accordingly, they consume a wide variety of self-reported data from surveys, panels, and similar sources. The advantage of attitudinal analytics is their ability to measure and forecast qualitative metrics such as brand awareness and purchase intent. They are also easier to execute than other forms of analysis such as behavioral analytics, since you do not have to work with your channel partners to collect this type of data.

The most common attitudinal analytics are based on the purchase funnel (see Exhibit 4-3), which has been taught in Marketing 101 for decades. The purchase funnel tracks customers from their first exposure to a brand or brand awareness down through successive levels, including opinion, purchase consideration, and purchase intention, until the purchase and repurchase levels are reached at the bottom of the funnel. The analytics at each level, often based upon customer surveys, indicate the likelihood that, for this particular product, customers will move down to the next level of the funnel, toward greater purchase probability and brand loyalty.

The levels of the funnel, as it is typically presented, sport generic titles. In actuality, they can be refined to encompass the whole battery of metrics that concern today's marketers. These include attitudinal measures such as brand and product image; net promoter scores; key questions such as, "Would you recommend the brand to a friend?"; and activity measures such as GRPs, leads developed, and dealer market share.

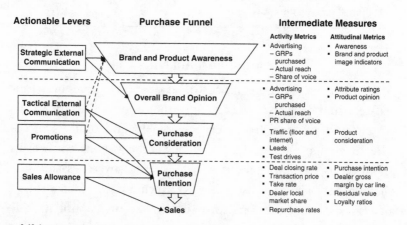

Exhibit 4-3 The Purchase Funnel and Its Levers and Measures

Attitudinal analytics, such as the purchase funnel, serve two purposes. First, they are diagnostic tools that measure the relationship between the brand and its current and targeted customers at a specific point in time. With this information, marketers can look at their "scores" for the different levels and identify the bottlenecks occurring in their brands. For instance, if a specific brand of car enjoys a consumer awareness score of 99 percent, but only 17 percent of consumers have a positive opinion of it, its marketers know where to focus their attention and spending on building the brand's reputation.

When combined with regression analysis, attitudinal analytics also enable marketers to predict how investments in certain levers (or marketing vehicles) will affect the level of the funnel at which they are aimed and the levels below it. For instance, the car marketers can use the funnel to predict what impact raising the brand's opinion score would have on purchase consideration or actual purchase.

Korea-based LG Electronics applied just such an analysis in its global digital appliance (DA) business. When LG DA wanted to better understand its marketing results in durable goods—washers/dryers and refrigerators—in three different countries (two developed nations and one developing nation), it turned to the purchase funnel. The funnel, with its levels and levers, served as a standard and consistent framework for assessing performance across countries. It also enabled the company to analyze spending and return at each stage of funnel by country, by product line, and by marketing vehicle.

The analysis revealed that in the first developed nation, LG DA could best improve its ROI by eliminating less productive spending lower in the funnel, such as in price reductions and rebates, to build familiarity and awareness higher in the funnel.

In the developing nation, the analysis suggested that investment be increased at the lower levels of funnel, in particular to building the capacity of the retail sales staff to better serve customers. And in the second developed nation, the analysis revealed that events aimed at increasing favorable brand associations and word of mouth among consumers would enhance the conversion from familiarity to consideration in the middle of funnel.

There are a variety of attitudinal analytics in use, but they are easy to identify because they are all fueled by self-reported data. Young & Rubicam Brand's BrandAsset Valuator (BAV) is a good example. The company bills BAV as the world's largest brand database, tracking 35,000 brands over 72 metrics, including brand health, consideration, and loyalty. BAV provides both measures and forecasts. Its key characteristic, however, is the source of the information used to populate the database—customers. In the United States, that data is collected "via a panel of over 13,000 respondents that is refreshed by new respondents quarterly."[8]

ANSWERING QUESTIONS WITH
THE PURCHASE FUNNEL

Purchase funnels help marketers answer a variety of questions. Here are some of the typical questions you can answer at each level:

- *Brand and product awareness.* How well do my marketing events capture the attention of the target consumers?
- *Familiarity/overall brand opinion.* What do the target consumers feel about my brand based on what they know?
- *Purchase consideration/intention/interest.* How successful are we at getting consumers to try the brand, whether it's a container of orange juice at the supermarket or a test drive at the dealership?

- *Sale/transaction*. How many more units do we sell as a direct result of a marketing event or series of events?
- *Loyalty/service/repurchase*. Was the experience such that our customers will come back for more, or were they just in it for the cheap price?

Business Case Analytics

Business case analytics are familiar to most marketers. These analytics require a minimum amount of data, which is usually available within the company. Typically, they are relatively uncomplicated and require only simple, "back-of-the-envelope" calculations. For these reasons, they are particularly useful when initial "reality checks" are needed, analytic capabilities are not yet fully developed, and/or other types of data are unavailable.

Breakeven analysis is a well-established and long-used business case analytic. It does not generate an ROI, but it does produce an upper and lower set of boundaries that marketers can use to weigh their investment decisions. There are many ways to use breakeven analysis depending on your industry, company, and market vehicles. In the following example, it was used because the financial data was incomplete and customer response data was unavailable.

Several years ago, a global wine and spirits distributor was spending significantly on on-premise promotional events. These events included lavish dinners for community "influencers," sampling promotions at working-class taverns, and everything in between. The problem was that each brand was running its own events in its own way, most with a seat-of-the-pants approach to measuring success. When asked about the effectiveness of an event, one salesperson said, "There were more than six hundred people at the event, and they were young and single and had money to burn." This was as specific as the responses got. Further, the sheer number of events they were overseeing daunted the brand managers themselves—one brand conducted nearly two hundred sampling events at bars and lounges in one month alone.

As disparate as the events were their goals were similar. They were all consumer-focused, high-touch events aimed at building awareness and recall among very focused targets. What they needed was order and rigor in their analytics.

The company imposed that by creating a database of event cost information and then used breakeven analysis—comparing the cost of the proposed event to the number of bottles of liquor the attendees would have to purchase to cover the investment—to evaluate their effectiveness. The results were eye opening. It turned out that the cost of these events varied widely, according to the venue itself and how elaborate the event's design. In the most extreme case, to payout the event (or make it break even), a participant would have to become a fan of the product and purchase no less than 80 bottles worth of the premium Scotch being promoted—more than most of the attendees would consume in several years or, in some cases, a lifetime.

By helping marketers understand how much volume an event would have to deliver in order to make financial sense, business case analytics allowed them to gauge their spending. As a result, about a fifth of the marketing budget at this wine and spirits distributor was reallocated to support events that were more profitable, and a 10 percent improvement in marketing effectiveness was captured.

CHOOSING AMONG ANALYTIC APPROACHES

A good way to visualize the three classes of analytics is to place them on a continuum, as in Exhibit 4-4. At the far end of the continuum are behavior analytics, which use actual customer responses to measure ROI and produce predictions. Attitudinal analytics occupy the center of the spectrum. They are less accurate and less ROI driven than behavioral analytics, but, at the same time, they allow marketers to understand brands more comprehensively. And back at the beginning of spectrum, there are business case analytics that don't require customer data or produce an ROI but that can be implemented with data that typically is close at hand.

In considering the analytics continuum, all marketers should aspire to behavior analytics as the gold standard. They produce measurements and predictions that are most intimately related to consumer purchase behavior and profitability. But marketers should recognize that there are times when modeling may not be the best or most viable way to analyze marketing efforts. For

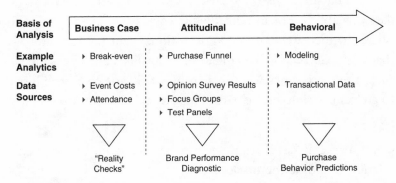

Exhibit 4-4 The Range of Marketing Analytics

instance, behavior analytics are not likely to be the best analytical approach when the data needed to fuel a model is not available, the marketing spend is not great enough to justify the cost of constructing a model, or the marketer is more focused on brand image than the bottom line (although the rationality of such an approach should be carefully considered). Accordingly, marketers must be able to choose among different analytical approaches or, better yet, enlist a battery of approaches that can provide a comprehensive set of quantitative and qualitative metrics for measuring brand performance.

Choosing among analytics requires that marketers consider three variables: data availability, internal capabilities, and brand objectives and vehicles.

Data Availability

All analytical approaches require data, and accordingly the first consideration in choosing among analytics is data availability. Then, reach for an analytical approach that comes the closest to customer purchase behavior.

ROI marketers also understand that there are limitations to data availability. For instance, when they are marketing a brand across 10 media channels or promotional vehicles, it is unlikely that they will be able to collect high-quality data across all 10. Also, there are times when it is too difficult or cost prohibitive to collect certain types of data. Thus, they start with three simple guidelines:

- If a marketer has or can get transactional data, behavior analytics should be the first choice.
- If transactional data is unavailable, but self-reported data is available, attitudinal analytics are indicated.

- If profitability and event cost data are the only data available, business case analytics may be the best option.

Internal Capabilities

The second consideration in choosing analytics is the internal capacity of the marketer's organization. The first pillar of marketing ROI encompasses complex and often unfamiliar work, and every company's analytical capacity is different.

The primary guideline for this variable is to start from where you are. For instance, there is no sense in collecting transactional data and choosing modeling as an analytical approach if your organization doesn't have the statistical expertise needed to build the model or the budget to buy one. Instead of trying to begin with a giant leap forward, aspiring ROI marketers often start with a smaller step and focus on analytical approaches that they have the expertise to execute right now as well as the vehicles that consume the largest portion of their marketing spend.

One of Latin America's leading beverage producers provides a good example of this guideline in action. The company is a major billboard advertiser, leasing approximately five thousand billboards at any one time. But calculating the ROI of billboards is very difficult. How many people were actually paying attention to them and how many were buying their beverage as result? The marketing team answered these questions by calculating GRPs for billboards—in some cases, actually counting the number of cars that drove by. Then, the company compared billboard GRPs to TV GRPs, and calculated the ROI of each of the billboards on that basis. When the results were plotted, the company was able to maximize its billboard ROI by deciding in each case whether to continue to advertise the specific brand in that location, whether to advertise a different brand in that location, or whether to abandon the location altogether. Secondarily, it started thinking and planning for the long term. Ask yourself what metrics you need to understand and which analytical approaches can provide insight into them. Begin to develop these analytics, perhaps by hiring outside expertise to help create them. Be aware, however, that the critical issues with analytics are reproducibility and reliability. The marketing ROI capability cannot be outsourced and eventually, even if calculations are outsourced, internal expertise will be needed to manage the process and ensure the quality of the outsourced service.

Brand Objectives and Vehicles

The third consideration in choosing analytical approaches is the marketing objectives for your brands. Ideally, marketers set brand objectives based on where the brand has evolved in its life cycle and then determine which vehicles can best achieve those objectives. Different vehicles produce different levels of data availability, require different levels of investment, and require the use of different analytical approaches.

For example, launching a new product typically requires large investments to build brand awareness. You would choose vehicles such as billboards, Web sites, and sponsorships in support of that goal and an analytical approach—probably the purchase funnel—that is focused on a qualitative metric. Conversely, if you were trying to boost purchase on a mature brand in a competitive market, you might choose consumer coupons, TV ads, or Internet direct sales and use an analytical approach—in this case, modeling—which measures purchase behavior more directly. In general terms, brand-building efforts that seek to affect customer perceptions generally suggest attitudinal analytics. Sales and volume-focused objectives generally suggest behavior analytics.

Ultimately, if you have all the data you need and the analytical expertise, you should use multiple analytical approaches whenever possible no matter what your brand objectives and marketing vehicles. Events designed to generate trial, for example, virtually always come with a negative ROI, but you should know how much money you are losing and limit those losses by choosing those trial events with "least-negative" ROIs whenever possible. Moreover, you should use business case analytics to determine whether the level of trial generated can create enough sales to pay back the cost of the investment over time. Conversely, it is entirely possible to run a brand into the ground by focusing solely on purchase without regard for qualitative metrics such as putting a designer handbag on sale every other week. So, in this case you would want to know what is happening in the purchase funnel as you drive sales.

In short, while we've offered practical shortcuts to start building the analytics pillar in this chapter, we are not suggesting that they can be permanent substitutes for a fully developed analytical prowess.

* * * *

Learning to use analytical approaches and the data that fuels them, the first pillar of the marketing ROI capability, enables marketers to begin stripping away the complexity around marketing spend and create a set of initial guidelines that can rationalize it. But no matter how rational and detailed, guidelines by their nature cannot be routinized, and, as the next chapter will show, they are inherently inaccurate. In other words, the analytical pillar alone is not sturdy enough to support the marketing ROI capability.

Marketing ROI also requires easy-to-use and intuitive decision support tools for applying the analytic approaches throughout the marketing organization, processes that ensure that the analytics and decisions support tools are fully utilized and that have the support and motivation from the company at large. In the next three chapters, we will show how those marketing ROI requisites—the remaining three pillars—are developed.

packages. Specialized software boutiques, such as M-Factor, MMA, and DemandTec, build stand-alone marketing DS tools. And, a few advanced marketing companies, such as Harrah's Entertainment, build proprietary tools.

Harrah's need for analytics and DS tools became urgent in the mid-1990s, when expansion opportunities dried up and competition within the gaming industry heated up. At that time, the company, under the leadership of then CEO Phil Satre, invested $30 million in the Winner Information Network (WINet) database. Built around Harrah's Total Rewards loyalty card, this database collected detailed information about the behavior and gambling results of the 16 million customers that the company had enlisted by that time. When WINet went live in February 1997, Harrah's was the only company in its industry to have a database that encompassed and integrated customer behavior across all of its properties.[1]

The only problem, Satre later explained, was that Harrah's "built an F-16, but forgot to train the pilots."[2] In 1998, he solved that problem in a surprising way. He hired Gary Loveman, a Harvard Business School professor, as Harrah's COO. An unlikely gambling czar, Loveman transformed Harrah's and eventually the entire gaming industry with his single-minded focus on marketing analytics. At the time, glitz was the driving force in the industry and casinos were attracting customers with roller coasters and volcanoes. "All I wanted to talk about was customer behavior," Loveman recalls. "Who's coming and who's not? We had the database to tell us this. Whose frequency is up, and whose frequency was down? Who's coming with an offer, and who's not coming with an offer? Who's coming on weekends, and who's coming on weekdays? Who's coming with a spouse, and who doesn't have a spouse? And how are these patterns changing? People weren't prepared for those discussions. They panicked."

The first thing Loveman did was to start developing the sophisticated analytical models needed to extract insights from Harrah's customer database. He also began creating DS tools that would enable Harrah's to transform the insights that the Rewards database yielded into working knowledge. "Nothing was off the shelf. We built all that stuff and still do," says Loveman, now Harrah's CEO and chairman. "I spend a lot of time on tool development. The company really depends on a set of intellectual assets—marketing being the primary, but there are others—and I spend a lot of time on the development of those tools."[3] These tools became the basis for a two-pronged marketing/service strategy.

First, Harrah's marketers used analytic tools to calculate the long-term profitability of each Total Rewards cardholder based on the frequency and volume of his or her gambling. Then, they modeled and ran events designed to attract the greatest number of high-value customers to the company's casinos.

Richard Mirman, who was a Booz Allen Hamilton consultant before serving consecutive stints as Harrah's VP of relationship marketing, CMO, and, until his resignation in mid-2007, senior vice president of new business development, explains:

> Our Harrah's property in Las Vegas is a converted Holiday Inn that sits across the street from a $1.8 billion property, but we generate more slot revenue than they do. How do we do this? Because Bellagio spent $1.8 billion to *attract* this customer to come stay with them. We built all this distribution and technology to *invite* this customer.
>
> We know that this customer from Joliet is worth $400 in gaming. So we're going to say, "You're in Las Vegas? You know

what, we're going to give you a free room." Now Bellagio, which has a nicer product, can't do that because they don't know that this customer is a $400 customer. They can't give away that room, otherwise there goes their entire business model. What they'll say is "Hey, we've got the best room, come and pay $150."

What you find is that, one, customers take our free room offer and, two, we know it costs, let's say, $50 to flip the room and we're picking up $350 for every hotel room that we give away because that customer generates at least $350 worth of gaming revenue. Now, if you multiply that by the 20-some-odd properties that are around and the 28 million customers, all of a sudden, it's a big, honking deal.

Second, once those customers arrive, Harrah's service reps and property staff members use DS tools to make sure those customers are treated to the highest service levels in the industry. In doing so, the company earns those customers' loyalty and a greater share of their gambling wallet. For instance, when customers telephone for reservations, those with higher "values" (that is, those whose behavior yields more profit over the long term) spend less time in phone queues than those with lower customer values. When customers are connected, Harrah's operators are prompted to offer better room rates to those callers with higher customer values. DS tools also enable Harrah's to choose which customers should be offered show tickets via their cell phones and to inform VIP hosts when to contact high-value customers who have been away too long and what to offer to them to entice them to return. In fact, Harrah's is actually harnessing behavioral data and making marketing decisions on the spin of the wheel; it tracks customers' gambling in real time, and if a customer's losses become excessive, a DS tool will prompt a floor employee to alleviate the sting by delivering a cash voucher or other gift on the spot.

The integration of marketing and service efforts helped Harrah's raise its share of its customers' gambling from 36 percent to 50 percent in less than a decade. "The marketing things were all inducements to loyalty," explains Loveman. "Then, you had to deliver an increasingly convincing service when you got the customer here to make the marketing stuff stick. And that's exactly what's driven the company. People have consolidated their business with us partly because the marketing is driving it here and partly because the service is supporting it. Those two things had to go hand in hand."

DS tools helped Harrah's develop both prongs of this strategy and capitalize on the richness of customer response data available in the gaming environment. In the process, Harrah's transformed itself from an also-ran in the 1990s into the largest player in the gaming industry. In 2006, its revenues approached $10 billion, and the company received and accepted a $17 billion buyout offer from two hedge funds.

WHY ROI MARKETERS NEED DECISION SUPPORT TOOLS

When the ways in which Harrah's and other ROI marketers use DS tools are examined, four benefits that explain why these tools are an integral structural component of the marketing ROI capability become clear:

1. They make sophisticated analytics accessible to nonspecialists.
2. They routinize analytics and thus help ensure rigor and consistency in the use of data.
3. They are adaptable, enabling employees to analyze the needs of specific markets, regions, customer segments, and individual customers.

4. They distribute the knowledge needed to make sound investment decisions to the proper levels within the company.

Accessibility

Decision support tools cut through the inherent complexity of analytics and enable companies to operationalize their marketing ROI capability. These tools are analogous to the operating systems on personal computers such as Microsoft Windows. An operating system is the "front end" that allows people who aren't computer scientists and programmers to manage and navigate through their computers. If you remember the days when a computer user needed to know how to write code to use the machine—or later, when the user had to learn many commands to use early operating systems such as QDOS, on which MS-DOS was based (and an acronym for Quick and Dirty Operating System, for good reason)—you know the importance of an accessible interface between people and computers. DS tools serve the same purpose—they are the user-friendly front end of the analytical engines that support marketing ROI.

In 1990, Booz & Company created one of the first DS tools for analytic planning in the consumer packaged goods industry for this very reason. We had constructed an analytical model for a client, but distributing its power to the sales force posed another problem. The model was too complicated and time-consuming for salespeople to use in the course of their everyday duties, and so they didn't. This is a problem common to all sophisticated analytics. If marketers need to create spreadsheets, enter more than a handful of numbers, or wait hours in a queue for results, or if they can't interpret those results, analytics won't get used.

Because there was no off-the-shelf solution to this problem available in 1990, we built Tradewins, a software program that allowed our client's salespeople to access the analytic engine and tap into its power in a few keystrokes. Tradewins and the many planning DS tools that are now available make using analytics for planning promotions easy and intuitive; they reduce the work of producing a plan to entering clearly identified data into a standardized form, which automatically produce outcome predictions and reports. DS tools, no matter whether their specific purpose is brand building, sales promotions, or customer service, are valuable for precisely that reason: they ensure that employees don't need advanced degrees in statistics to use analytics, and they broaden and deepen the applications of analytics, even when practiced by people who are already proficient at them.

Routinization

When analytics are not run with rigor and consistency, the answers they produce can be unintentionally, and sometimes intentionally, misleading (see Chapter 4). This outcome becomes even more likely when people must create and run their own spreadsheets in order to access the insights that analytics produce. Typically, variations pop up in the construction of each spreadsheet and in the data used to populate them. As a result, the answers that they produce are neither accurate nor comparable.

DS tools ensure efficient and effective results by routinizing the analytics. In terms of efficiency, these tools streamline marketing processes and enable marketers to act quickly. In terms of effectiveness, the tools take an analytical equation and run it thousands of times with many different combinations of data, but always in a consistent way. Thus, salespeople and marketers can plan, execute, and evaluate the effectiveness of their events across brands, geographies, and vehicles and get an apples-to-apples comparison.

The Latin-American beverage producer, introduced in the previous chapter, provides a good example of the value of such comparisons. As we've already said, the company created an apples-to-apples ROI comparison between billboard advertising and TV, but marketing analysis actually went much further than that. In fact, it created comparable ROIs across of all its marketing vehicles, including media such as TV, billboard, radio, and print; price and promotion such as trade discounts and loyalty programs; sporting events such as bullfights; and point of sales such as merchandising, shelf space positioning, and demo girls. And then the company reallocated its marketing spend based on the findings. The result of this work is that the company reversed its market share slide and regained its leading 70 percent share in its market.

Adaptability

In 2007, according to *CIA World Factbook*, the average fertility rate for American women was 2.09 children. Many companies think in averages, too. They know the cost of acquiring the average customer, how much that average customer spends, and how long they retain that average customer.

Unfortunately, while these averages are useful for summarizing vast amounts of data, they can be the bane of sound marketing decisions. The problem is that 2.09 children have never stepped out of anyone's minivan and the *average* customer rarely buys anything. Instead, there are parents who shop for one child and others who shop for four children, and their spending habits are very different. What's right on average is wrong almost everywhere.

Moreover, the deviations from the average can make or break marketing efforts; hence, the value of DS tools: they enable marketers to think about and act on the specifics that distinguish actual individual customers. This might mean changing vehicles based on the product such as using the Internet to provide the content-rich marketing that customers look for when they shop for durable appliances or mobile to deliver a coupon for a fast-food restaurant as customers are going to lunch in California. It could also mean changing the marketing mix across the world. Take one global consumer products company that traditionally has been a mass media advertiser. As increasing numbers of its customers have begun spending more and more of their time online, this company has aggressively built its online marketing presence. But that shift did not make sense in Mexico, one of the company's most profitable markets, because the Internet infrastructure and access in that nation has not yet developed to the same degree as in the United States and other nations. The DS tools they employ have helped them focus their media investments differently in different markets.

Part and parcel of the adaptability engendered by DS tools is the "what-if" capability they offer marketers. What if we reduce the budget by 10 percent in Japan and add it to India? What if we reduce print by 7 percent and add it to in-store media? In the marketers' ability to answer such questions, DS tools enable fast, accurate scenario planning.

Distributed Decision Making

In addition to thinking in averages, many companies also make marketing decisions at the wrong levels. Often, the results of marketing programs vary by geographic, demographic, and psychographic attributes. And just as often, decisions made at headquarters do not adequately account for those variations. Conversely, not all decisions should be made locally. Some degree of centralization and standardization is necessary. You need to define the parameters within which people are allowed to make decisions so that the responsibility flows to wherever it is needed to ensure that sound investment decisions can be made.

As a rule, *decisions need to be made at the level at which you are capturing the most value.* If a company is running a sampling program, for example, hundreds of people should be making many decisions at local levels such as what times to conduct the events, where to position the event within the stores, and how much to pay the staff. Conversely, decisions about the content and time slots for a national TV spot may require the involvement of only five or six people and should be made at corporate headquarters.

What does this mean in practice? It depends on the particulars of your decision-making process and the differentiation in your markets. But generally speaking, as companies decentralize marketing decisions, those decisions become increasingly precise. However, there is also a cost and an effort involved in decentralizing decisions, and eventually a point of diminishing returns is reached. So the objective is to push decisions down to the point where the returns outweigh the costs and effort—but no further than that.

DS tools enable companies to deploy the knowledge and the power needed to make effective decisions at the proper levels within the organization. They put the power to customize the marketing mix for brands based on customer response in the hands of brand and field marketers, salespeople, and customer service reps. At the same time, they ensure that marketing events are tailored to individual accounts and customers *within* corporate guidelines that have been designed to maintain brand standards and messages.

DECISION SUPPORT TOOLS APPLIED

There are three principle applications of DS tools: planning, execution, and post-event analysis and tracking (PEAT). Planning tools are "what if" oriented; they help marketers decide what to do. Execution tools are "what is" oriented; they help marketers ensure that what they plan to do is actually done. And PEAT tools are "what-was" oriented; they measure results and surface the causes of any deviation from the expected results.

In a ideal world, all three types of DS tools would be working together to form a complete set of enabling tools—a marketing ROI system that helps close the marketing loop and drives profitability. In practice, it takes a fair amount of deliberate design to integrate them. Even without full integration, the value of the tools is considerable. To illustrate that value, consider the following case study revealing how these tools are used at Epsilon Foods (a real company with a disguised name). Epsilon is a major player in the canned and frozen-food industry, which realized savings on its promotional spending of $100 million annually after equipping its sales force with these tools.

Planning Tools

Planning tools help marketers create events that will connect with customers and meet the targets their companies set for them. These tools accomplish these goals by enabling marketers to build events in different ways, predict their outcomes, and identify those events that feature the most desirable outcomes *before* they invest their resources. In short, planning tools are used to optimize the allocation of resources.

Epsilon Foods built its planning tool in order to properly allocate and optimize its trade and consumer promotion spending. The tool allows an Epsilon salesperson to create her own "library" of hypothetical events (each featuring different price points, display levels, products, timing, duration, and so on) for each of her accounts, calculate the predicted incremental volume and ROI of each proposed event, and rank the events by their predicted profitability. So, for a can of beans, for instance, the salesperson might compare the different sales and profit outcomes produced by lowering the price, buying a display, running the product in a circular ad, or creating a shopper card offer.

Once the "best" event is identified (the event with the highest ROI given the objectives for the brand), the Epsilon salesperson conducts a reality check to confirm that this event can be executed as planned. At Epsilon, that might mean that the retailer is willing to participate given the proposed parameters or that the event fits into the retailer's overall promotion calendar given its commitments to other manufacturers. With the results of this check in hand, the salesperson adjusts the event parameters as needed and uses the tool to recalculate the incremental volume and ROI. Then, the proposed event is finalized and added to the salesperson's event calendar and overall plan.

When the salesperson's plan for the coming period is complete, it is "published." In other words, it is formalized, and its overall volume and ROI are recorded, so that others in the company have access to the consolidated account plan. This plan is added to the plans from the rest of the sales force, which management can review, compare to the targets that have been established for its consumer and trade promotion budgets for that particular planning period, and, if necessary, adjust them.

Epsilon used its planning tool for promotions, but there are planning tools that cast a wider net—tools that can be applied across the marketing mix, whether it be conventional vehicles such as TV and print, or one of the new media vehicles that have emerged in recent years such as mobile messaging or search. In each case, planning tools guide marketers by calculating overall marketing spend outcomes, the optimal marketing levers, and variations in the market impact of events designed with differing sets of parameters.

Execution Tools

Execution tools help marketers in three ways. They ensure that what marketers plan is what they get—that Internet banner ads are placed on the sites the marketer specified, that TV ads appear in the frequency and time slots the agency or media company purchased, or that the promotional offers sold into a retailer are properly delivered. They feed the execution data needed for payment and post-event analysis through the marketing ROI system. And they can even enable marketers to make midcourse corrections aimed at improving their event results while they are occurring.

When the actual results of analytics-powered marketing plans do not materialize as expected, the cause of the performance deviation is very often found in the execution of the events. For example, after the CEO of a consumer products company repeatedly complained that the only time he saw his company's TV ads was after midnight, the marketing department had the ads tracked and discovered he was right. The advertising plan had called for specific weekend, daytime, and near–prime time hours, but, in fact, many of the ads were running in less-than-desirable time slots. And, of course, they were not producing the incremental volume and ROI numbers that the company's marketing mix models had predicted. The cause of the problem was simple: the ad campaign was a large one, and when the company's outsourced media buyers could not purchase ad space in the desired time slots, they took whatever slots were available. The media buyers invoiced the company in bulk and the company paid the invoice without knowing whether or not its plan had been properly executed. This is the kind of problem that execution tools are designed to surface. They provide constant and consistent feedback about whether or not you are doing what you said you would do and getting what you are buying.

Execution tools also play an essential role in transmitting critical event data into the marketing ROI system. As events occur, their actual costs and other related data is entered in the tool. This triggers payment approvals and provides an essential set of data required to calculate ROI in the post-event analysis.

At Epsilon Foods, the execution tool was packaged with its planning tool and connected directly to the company's enterprise software and accounts payable function. This event data was passed from the planning tool to the execution system, and the salesperson then triggered payment by taking any required adjustments and submitting approval to accounts payable. (A notable feature of Epsilon's execution tool was that a salesperson could not trigger payment for an event unless and until it had been published in the planning tool. In this way, the execution tool itself reinforced the sales force's acceptance and use of the company's marketing ROI system.)

Currently, execution tools are merging with post-event analysis and tracking tools, which facilitates midcourse corrections in marketing programs. One example is the latest crop of ad optimizers offered by companies such as Ogilvy North America. These tools use the behavior of viewers to automatically adjust online display ads, which accounted for $15.7 billion in marketing spending in 2006, in order to enhance response. If an ad in one color isn't attracting enough attention from online viewers, the tool will change the ad's color. "We've reached the point of instantaneous feedback," says Ogilvy co-CEO Carla Hendra.[4]

Post-event Analysis and Tracking Tools

The final category of DS tools contains post-event analysis and tracking (or PEAT) tools. PEAT tools facilitate the analysis of event outcomes, create the learning that is required to improve analytics and enhance results moving forward, and produce reports that disseminate this knowledge to the people who need it to enhance the company's marketing results.

Just as planning tools make predictive analytics easy and intuitive to use, PEAT tools make historical analytics easy and intuitive. Financial and event data from the execution system are combined with external data from third parties such as IRI, JD Power, and ACNielsen and run through the ROI formula. In other words, they determine the actual profitability of events and pull other information to judge the success of an event or a collection of events that together comprise the advertising program—knowledge that, as discussed in Chapter 1, many marketers do not currently have at their disposal. (In addition to informing managers of results, these outcomes are stored as part of an event database, which can be accessed to create lessons learned from a large sample of events.)

PEAT tools don't stop there. They also collect the event predictions created by planning tools and compare them to the actual event outcomes. This brings to the surface discrepancies in performance and enables marketers, usually with the help of the statisticians, to diagnose and eliminate the causes of those discrepancies.

When the information produced by PEAT tools is applied to the marketing process, the marketing process becomes a closed learning loop and marketing improvement becomes continuous. When the information produced by PEAT tools is applied to the improvement of the model itself, the next round of event planning becomes more accurate and more successful.

Typically, PEAT tools automatically generate a suite of reports that disseminate this knowledge. These reports deliver relevant knowledge in an easy-to-digest form to various levels within the company. Some of these reports summarize tactical knowledge for employees in the field; others aggregate results for product managers; and still others offer senior managers the broad metrics they need to determine whether and how well the company's marketing strategy is being executed.

Back at Epsilon Foods, there was plenty of performance data available but no way for salespeople to broadly and consistently apply it until the company created its own PEAT tool. The new tool pulled incremental volume and merchandising conditions from ACNielsen, trade spend and contribution margin data from the financial system, shipment data from an internal customer data warehouse, and account plans from the planning tool.

Epsilon's PEAT tool automatically aligned all this data at the event level and calculated performance metrics such as shipment contribution, ROI, and actual shipments versus plan. It identified performance shortfalls, which statisticians helped salespeople and their managers analyze and address. The PEAT tool outputs were used to identify best practices, which were shared throughout the sales force and improved the pricing and promotion planning process. (There is nothing like seeing actual results to help make next year's planning decisions better.) Further, for the first time, sales and marketing executives at company headquarters began to receive aggregated performance metrics that enabled them to access the effectiveness of their promotional spending. Using them, the executives were able to determine which promotions worked, which accounts and channels were most profitable and deserved more spending, and which brands could sustain more marketing (not just pricing and promotion) investment. Like planning tools, PEAT tools can be applied to any event in which the data needed to evaluate ROI is available. These tools can tell marketers how their execution and performance compares to their plans, reveal the causes of variation, and, in doing so, provide direction for corrective actions across the marketing mix.

ERECTING THE DECISION SUPPORT TOOL PILLAR

Marketers face a number of choices as they approach the development of the second pillar of the marketing ROI capability. For one, they must decide on a source for their tools. The major enterprise software vendors offer DS tools as integrated components of their systems, but these usually come with some trade-off in customization and functionality. Boutique developers are pushing the envelope and creating more sophisticated tools, but they tend to be dedicated to specific applications, and integration with enterprise and legacy systems can become an issue. Marketers can build their own, as Harrah's has, but that requires a level of expertise and investment in time and resources that can be prohibitive in many companies—especially considering the required maintenance over time.

Marketers must also decide on the range and depth of the tool. DS tools like those used by Epsilon Foods for promotion and pricing are relatively common. But for other vehicles, particularly in some of the harder-to-measure opportunities offered in new media (such as a corporate presence on Facebook), tools are just being created. These new tools incorporate models that are pushing the predictive edge of analytics by measuring the activity that a Web site or a video is creating across the Internet and statistically correlating that activity to sales.

Then, there is also the question of whether the tool will encompass multiple vehicles. Marketing mix tools, declared the ANA Accountability Task Force, "represent a quantum leap in marketing efficiency and are correctly viewed as one of the two or three major developments in the history of marketing."[5] As desirable and important as it is to capture the impact of various vehicles side by side and optimize your investments in them, marketing mix tools are not an end in and of themselves and need to be weighed against the investment required to acquire these tools and their potential for return. You should only build a routinized system when your spending is large enough to justify the investment in the analytics and DS tools, which may not always be the case with all of your marketing vehicles.

Finally, there is the question of integration. When we described the tree principle applications of DS tools, we talked about a set of tools that is integrated into a complete system. Ideally, planning, execution, and PEAT tools would be fully integrated with each other. Data and results would flow seamlessly from one application to the next and the system's users could access and move among the tools from one screen. In reality, that level of integration can be ongoing challenge for even the most advanced ROI marketers.

So, how you should navigate these choices? As with analytics, take small steps first. Start with a planning tool that addresses your largest marketing spend "bucket." Even if the tool is not perfect, it should be able to deliver a positive effect on the ROI of your events relatively quickly. If you have existing CRM tools, which many companies have already integrated in their enterprise software, consider whether you can deploy it more fully or customize it. If you do not have an existing planning tool, survey the standalone tools on the market. If you don't need a high level of customization, buy one off the shelf. If you need a customized tool, hire a boutique firm to build one or, if you can, build it in-house. Put it to work. (Do beware that this is just a starting point; the effort will fall apart unless you take the next step to routinize the process and lock it in organizationally.)

Once you have demonstrated success, start expanding in two directions. First, add the execution and PEAT tools. In order to maximize the positive impact on ROI, you need to close the marketing loop—ensuring that ROI outcomes are tracked, measured, and used to drive improvement. Next, add depth to your planning tool; that is, incorporate your next largest bucket of spending and then the next and the next ... until the size of the next bucket does not justify the cost of the tool.

✳ ✳ ✳ ✳

With the first two pillars of the marketing ROI capability in place, you are armed with the analytics and the DS tools needed to determine marketing results and utilize them to build profitable volume. But if you stop at this point, you will not be able to activate the capability fully. In the next two chapters, we will discuss the final two pillars—process and organizational alignment. These are the two pillars that are forgotten most often, but they also are the pillars that transform marketing ROI into an organizational capability and ensure that companies can harness their full potential.

Chapter 6

Creating Process-Driven Profitability

Except for a brief period in the 1990s when reengineering was all the rage, business process management has rarely been thought of as exciting work. Nevertheless, thanks to the influence of quality experts like W. Edwards Deming, we all know that process plays a leading role in performance. Deming, who introduced companies the world over to statistical process control, is widely credited with saying, "If you can't describe what you are doing as a process, you don't know what you are doing."

The vast majority of marketing organizations already have processes in place. These processes control their workflow. Marketers use them to set goals, budget, plan, price, review, and so on. Typically, these processes are discrete; they are neither connected to each other nor in a closed loop. Thus, there is no assurance that they are working together and toward congruous, mutually consistent targets; that they will ever improve; or, in many cases, that their individual targets have been achieved. Often, they are neither recognized nor managed as processes—they have sprung up naturally in response to specific needs such as the need for managerial approval over spending.

The third pillar of marketing ROI resolves all of these problems by defining the when, where, and how of marketing processes in relation to each other, as well as incorporating analytics and DS tools into the marketing cycle. When the third pillar is in place, processes become the mortar that binds the other pillars of marketing ROI into an integrated system and fully realized capability.

Marketing ROI is composed of four processes—no more, no less. They are (as described in Chapter 3):

- *Target setting*, which enables marketers to set realistic goals, define the right set of metrics for measuring them, and cascade those goals down to the proper levels of the organization
- *Planning*, which allocates resources to offers, programs, and campaigns that are then delivered through various vehicles (for example, TV, Internet, mobile) to groups of consumers, and result in predicted volume and ROI outcomes
- *Execution*, which ensures that events happen as planned and creates the flexibility to respond quickly to changing circumstances
- *Post-event analysis*, which measures results (ideally, at the event level), surfaces the root causes of the differences between expected and actual outcomes, and captures the lessons that will improve outcomes in the future

So what makes these four processes different from the typical marketing processes that are already in place in most companies?

They are comprehensive and linked to each other in a closed loop, which creates shared goals, enables fact-based decision making, and enhances accountability. When processes are not integrated, accountability can be avoided even in the best of companies. Explains Clayton C. Daley Jr., vice chairman and CFO at P&G: "The old game around here was: 'If I'm a brand manager, my job is to sell my project to management and hope I've moved on the next job before the results come in.'"[1]

In marketing ROI, however, the integrated nature of the four processes, as shown in Exhibit 6-1, is a key ingredient in the

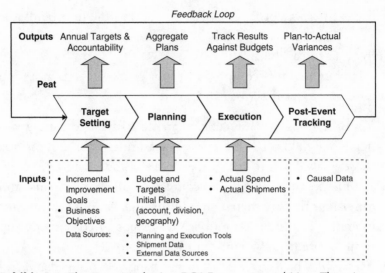

Exhibit 6-1 The Four Marketing ROI Processes and How They Are Linked through the PEAT Feedback Loop

creation of disciplined behavior and accountability, two prerequisites for goal achievement. Goals must be articulated, plans to achieve them created, plans executed, and outcomes measured and analyzed. In marketing ROI, these tasks are linked together, so marketers can be held accountable for their performance as well as learn from their mistakes and improve their performance and profitability over time. As Daley says, "If you've got a rigorous system, which we do now, of going back and evaluating your batting average on these projects, and hold the management accountable—not just the general management but the functional management in these business units—then you've got a system that is very self-correcting."[2]

A second characteristic of the four processes is shared goals. Ask marketing and field sales managers about their targets; the longer they spend rummaging around their offices in search of this year's operating plan, the longer the odds become that the targets featured in that plan will be met. Or worse, the better the odds that the company has marketing processes with contradictory targets.

Conversely, the targets that are set in marketing ROI's first process are deployed throughout the entire loop and cascade down to appropriate levels of the marketing organization, that is, where the greatest decision-making value can be captured. This ensures that marketers' efforts are all directed toward the same priorities and targets, raising the odds of successfully achieving them. This systematic deployment of goals is similar in intent to *hoshin kanri*, a strategic planning methodology created by Yoji Akao and used at companies such as Toyota. Toyota uses *hoshin* planning to ensure that corporate quality objectives are properly interpreted and deployed at multiple levels within the organization from the executive suite down to the plant floor. Cascading objectives is a proven and structured way to ensure that goals are distributed and shared across the company.[3]

The third characteristic of marketing ROI processes is that they are fact based. Far too often, marketing processes are governed by intuition. The most common example of this occurrence is when executives unilaterally decide marketing targets. When this happens, the targets are not tempered by the realities of the marketplace. An executive might say, "We hit $500 million last year and the CEO is calling for 10 percent growth, so the target is $550 million this year." The problems: there is no way of knowing whether the targets are attainable, and, even if they are, when the marketing managers (or other employees) believe that targets cannot be realistically achieved, they tend to neither take the targets seriously nor invest much effort in producing plans to achieve them.

Conversely, predictive models can tell marketers how many more sales they can expect if they spend x more dollars on product Y with vehicle Z. Thus, the targets, plans, actions, and analyses produced by these processes are built on reality. In marketing ROI, analytics are applied in each of the four processes, and process results are scientifically, consistently, and reliably measured.

Perhaps most important, the processes are well timed. Although the need for appropriate timing may seem obvious, mistimed marketing processes are very common. One of the reasons why the consumer products company described in the last chapter whose TV ads were running in the middle of the night could not buy the proper time slots was because its execution process was not sequenced properly. In fact, the company's budget process was so slow that by the time they finally committed to buy the time slots, the desired inventory had already been sold to other advertisers. Annual strategic targets set after the fiscal year has begun are another common example of timing gone awry.

In marketing ROI processes, the right timing ensures the effectiveness of targets, plans, actions, and analyses. The processes are properly synchronized with one another. (After all, planning without a target or acting without a plan results in a random walk without a destination.) And the timing within individual processes is properly scheduled and coordinated. One obvious example: the media buying that takes place in the execution process is timed to coincide with the seasonal sales schedules of the media companies.

Integrated, driven by shared goals, fact based, and properly timed—these are the characteristics that the four marketing ROI processes have in common. Keep these qualities in mind; the following sections will further define how each of the processes contributes to the quest for profitable volume.

THE TARGET-SETTING PROCESS

The target-setting process provides a set of common and fully articulated goals that are deployed throughout the entire marketing function and its work cycle. Once these targets are established, they also serve as beacon lights that guide the remaining three processes. In other words, the attainment of the targets is always the impetus behind the rest of the marketer's work.

The explicit targets set in a marketing ROI system compel action and propel the organization forward. When marketing's targets are set at meaningful levels above previous results, they force the organization out of its established patterns and set it in pursuit of innovation in all of its many forms. In most cases, the incremental improvement levels set by your marketing targets should be substantial enough to ensure that employees cannot achieve them by doing the same things that they have done in the past. This is the path to substantive change and continuous improvement.

In addition to creating forward momentum, the target-setting process provides two additional benefits. First, it requires that marketing's leadership team truly understand the company's objectives and boil them down to the right set of targets. Second, it ensures that those targets cascade down to the proper levels within the organization.

The Right Targets

One thing the most successful CMOs and other top marketers have in common is that they set "smart" targets. That is, they start with corporate objectives and drill down through them to brand objectives and then, to a set of metrics that accurately reflect those objectives (the measures that make up marketing dashboards and scorecards), and finally to a set of targets for reaching the objectives. In this way, these marketing leaders ensure that the targets they set for their organizations are aligned to the rest of the company.

Here's how Rob Malcolm describes the process at U.K.-based Diageo:

> We have scaled up our ambition and investment in innovation, and we've also scaled up our delivery in innovation. A significant portion of our growth this year came from products that we weren't marketing three years ago.
>
> Before metrics, we establish top- and bottom-line goals for innovation. We ask, What is it we want innovation to deliver? What's the contribution that we need to get out of innovation to support the growth we want as a company? And our answer has been very clear: By the end of five years, £1 billion [US$2 billion] of incremental net sales volume.
>
> We start with the financial contribution simply because if there weren't a positive effect on shareholder value, then why would we do it? Underneath that goal, we develop a strategy by asking, Where are we going to put our innovation priorities? Where are we going to mine? Where are we going to put our resources geographically? We talk about category, brand, product type, and technology.
>
> How should we allocate resources? What do we do to manage the pipeline? What's the hit rate we need to meet?

The "right" targets vary based on many factors including corporate objectives, the brand, budget, and so on. Typically, however, targets should always include ROI and specify both attitudinal measures, such as trial and awareness, and behavioral measures, such as incremental volume. Thus, targets are fully articulated goals in and of themselves.

The Right Levels

Setting targets is all well and good, but they mean different things at different levels of the organization. For one thing, they become more specific and action oriented as they reach the frontlines. Vice President of Brand Communications Olaf Göttgens explains how that works at Mercedes-Benz Passenger Cars, a division of DaimlerChrysler AG:

> We monitor the return on all of our marketing investments with a complex set of key performance indicators at every stage of the sales process. We set targets in advance and ask, "What do I want to achieve?" This can apply to very specifically defined measures. For instance: my target is to achieve 150 test drives a day, because I know that Mercedes-Benz has a conversion rate of 80 percent. That happens much less frequently with our competitors. So it makes sense for us to focus on getting people into the car.
>
> We set up in front of large hotels or at highway gas stations and invite people to drive the car to the next gas station. Or we'll have a presence at a resort where a manager might vacation with his family. It's successful because our prospects have the time in these settings to try out a new car. And those tryouts lead to brand/product experiences.[4]

Targets flow down through the organization as far as they need to go to enable effective decision making. Once they reach those levels, they are reinterpreted to ensure that they properly reflect local realities. This step is necessary because, for instance, a target for brand profitability may be an unrealistic expectation for a marketer who is introducing a new brand in a competitive market. At the same time, that same target may be far too modest for the manager whose brand is gaining momentum and market share in a different country. So, each will have a different profitability target, which will deliver the overall goal in aggregate.

The target-setting process transforms objectives into tangible targets, drives targets to the proper levels of the organization, and enables high-value decision making. But what makes a target-setting process viable? There are three qualities:

1. *In viable target-setting processes, decisions are made from the top down* and *the bottom up.* Too often, marketing targets are treated as top-down mandates. The senior marketing team decides what goals it wants and needs to accomplish in the coming period and simply imposes them on the product and field organizations. The problem, which is exacerbated as companies grow larger, is that leaders often are unaware of both local conditions and the trade-offs required to achieve their targets. This is why ROI marketers determine targets in a fashion that is simultaneously top down and bottom up. The "top" sets the targets, and the "bottom" provides feedback as to their viability. In this way, the act of target setting is an iterative process that incorporates the local conditions and the business trade-offs to set more robust and realistic goals. This process also promotes accountability on the part of marketers, who now have a say in the setting of the target; just as important, through their contribution, they have explicitly accepted responsibility for achieving it. This process also prevents people from "gaming" the system, because analytics expose unrealistic goals and puts checks and balances in place to challenge such goals. For instance, if management sets an overinflated "stretch" target, it provides sound grounds for a challenge if it is an impossible target; likewise, if people in the field underestimate the potential for growth to eliminate work or earn bonuses more easily, management has a means to discover the ploy.

2. *Viable target-setting processes specify resources.* All marketing requires an investment in resources, but often we see marketers being assigned targets that do not specify the money, knowledge, tools, or processes required to attain them. Sometimes this happens because targeting processes and budgeting processes are not integrated. Sometimes, it happens because executives set targets without considering how they will be achieved. The problem, of course, is that an improvement in results cannot happen without a corresponding change in resources. Thus, a target that requires an improvement in results without specifying the resources needed to attain it is suspect.

3. *Viable target-setting processes clearly assign responsibility for achieving the target.* As the saying goes, there is no *I* in team, but every team member still needs to pull his or her individual weight. Broad targets that don't specify individual goals, as in "we will raise the ROI of our print advertising by 10 percent," work for senior marketing executives, but are far too easy for employees at lower levels to shrug off. Viable target setting assigns responsibility in specific terms and in the context of the processes through which they will be attained. Thus, a specific brand manager's individual goal against the larger goal of a 10 percent increase in print ROI might state that "we will raise the ROI of the next print campaign for this brand by 15 points because when we tested this event, we gained 25 points, and now we will run in the entire target market."

THE PLANNING PROCESS

In general, marketing planning is an underdeveloped and less-than-rigorous process. The reasons for this happening vary.

Sometimes, marketing leaders mistakenly believe that setting and publicizing a target is tantamount to articulating how it will be achieved. Of course, that is not so. A *target* is an end; a *plan* is the means of reaching that end.

Another major reason for inadequate planning processes is the sheer number of possibilities and decisions entailed in a rigorous plan. Some marketing organizations deal with this complexity by centralizing decisions. For instance, they will plan their pricing based on a weighted average national level across all the channels, even though, as we have seen, the resulting average price is the wrong price virtually everywhere.

Sometimes, marketers deal with complexity by oversimplifying the process. They look at last year's plan and this year's targets and simply extrapolate: "we have 10 percent more to invest, so we'll add 10 percent across the existing mix," or "we got lots of hits from search, but that sponsorship didn't seem to do much. So, let's take 30 percent from sponsorships and give it to search." In each case, suboptimal returns are virtually guaranteed.

Instead of finding ways to duck the complexities of planning, ROI marketers embrace and manage it with the help of analytics and DS tools. Analytics-based planning tools enable marketers to quickly and easily calculate the results of hypothetical plans. These tools make managing complexity simple *and* raise predictive accuracy simultaneously.

In a marketing ROI system, the planning process begins before the target-setting process is over. This is because the "bottom-up" component of setting targets requires that marketers create and run hypothetical plans to determine if the proposed target is feasible. Once the initial target is finalized and accepted, planning begins in earnest.

The formalized targets that are generated in the first process of marketing ROI become the driving force of the planning process. In fact, the objective of this process is to transform targets into action plans. In order to accomplish this goal, marketers must decide how they will invest the money that they have been given to achieve their targets. Thus, plans are a series of resource allocation maps created at different levels with the marketing function.

Generally speaking, the planning process starts by taking the overall budget established in the target-setting process and allocating it by brand. Then, individual brand spending is allocated by geography. Then, spend is allocated by vehicle or by account.

For example, in a global company whose structure includes a CMO, global and local brand managers, field marketers, and a sales force that is responsible for trade promotions, the process might play out as follows:

- At the headquarters level, the CMO creates a plan that optimizes spending across the company's brands.
- Global managers create plans that allocate and optimize their portion of the spend across geographies.
- Local brand managers create plans that allocate their spending across vehicles.
- Field marketers and salespeople create individual plans that allocate their spending across events and accounts.

There might also be additional plans for centralized marketing efforts, such as corporate image building, which also must allocate spending over geographies and vehicles. So this planning process produces plans upon plans, each of which must sort through a seemingly infinite number of possibilities. But, of course, ROI marketers have the advantage of analytics and DS tools to manage the complexity.

This may seem like a straightforward planning cascade, but it requires a robust process that ensures that marketers run enough hypothetical plans to enable informed discussions around trade-offs at a variety of levels and discover the plan that offers the best overall returns. One major pharmaceuticals company took a creative approach to stimulating its planning process by auctioning off its marketing spend. It set up a "free market" for funding in which marketers competed by bidding with volume and profit results. The winning bids were the plans that promised the highest returns. Interestingly, this process forced efficiency on the entire system. Marketers who underestimated their predicted results in order to ease the performance burden and those who overestimated predicted results in order to gain funds were both forced to rework their bids when faced with more realistic, competing bids.

Before the planning process is complete, a reconciliation occurs. With the help of planning tools, all of the plans and their results are brought together. The aggregate results are checked against marketing's overall targets to ensure that, within the parameters of the company's marketing and brand strategies, they are realistic and meet their targets. The value of this process is the way in which it brings people together to evaluate marketing decisions and trade-offs around resource allocation.

THE EXECUTION PROCESS

In the third process of a marketing ROI system, action plans are transformed into action. This is the process in which marketers buy the advertising and sell-in and run promotions; they put the artwork on the bus and they call Google and Yahoo! to buy banner ad space. On its surface, execution is a straightforward process with which every marketer should be very familiar. It becomes more problematic, however, when events are not executed according to plan, a far-from-uncommon state of affairs.

There is also some complexity in the process that derives from the fact that different vehicles are purchased and executed in different ways. For instance, some vehicles, such as TV advertising or sponsorships, feature events that are purchased in bulk and up front. Other types of vehicles are purchased and executed over extended periods of time (for example, direct mail, trade promotions, and other events that companies control and direct internally).

A robust execution process has three primary objectives:

1. *Ensure that marketers actually get whatever it is that they are paying for.* In a sponsorship, for instance, that might mean verifying that the signage is properly posted or that a celebrity spokesperson hit the proper copy points. The execution process, with the help of DS tools, addresses these issues by tracking events as they happen and reconciling them against their plans and targets.

2. *Maintain the flexibility and creativity needed to change events in midcourse.* As marketers track events, especially those in which spending is extended over the course of a campaign, responses can be quickly measured and/or offers easily adjusted; they can sometimes find unexpected opportunities to improve outcomes. For instance, if a coupon or rebate that is being run for six weeks is being overredeemed after one week, its face value can be reduced over the next five weeks. An execution process that allows midcourse adjustments enables marketers to enhance profitability on the run.

    In addition, innovative solutions to execution problems are almost always possible. For example, one company that advertised heavily, and effectively, in print forced its marketers, whenever the company's profit targets were in jeopardy, to reduce print spending across the board to make its numbers. But after studying the problem, the company found that it could save 30 percent through supplier discounts by maintaining its current spend and promising to pay for 70 percent of the media up front. The new cost structure eliminated the quarterly disruptions; ROI improved and long-term brand equity was protected.

3. Collect data around the actual event—its costs and timing, as well as the associated volume and sales prices. In the fourth and final process, this information, after being run through analytics, enables marketers to determine the actual outcomes of their events.

THE POST-EVENT ANALYSIS PROCESS

The fourth and final process of a marketing ROI system, post-event analysis, ensures that event results are measured in a timely, relevant, and accurate manner. The biggest problem that marketers face with regards to post-event analysis is that they just don't do it. In neglecting the measurement of past results, it becomes more difficult to predict and improve their future results. This is a critical shortcoming of many companies. As more and more companies adopt marketing analytics and begin to use them to measure results and improve outcomes, those who do not do so are increasingly disadvantaged.

Timeliness dictates that post-event analysis is conducted as soon as it is feasible. In fact, a few ROI marketers measure results in real time and use those results to alter events while they are still occurring. Relevance dictates that the right metrics be measured.

This means that quantitative measures, such as incremental volume and ROI, receive as much attention as qualitative measures. Accuracy dictates that results are measured in a consistent and rigorous way. Consistency enables comparability, which in turn, allows sound allocation decisions; rigor means that everyone has to measure results and live by the consequences. Conversely, inaccurate results produce false interpretations. And if marketers don't trust results, they will not utilize them.

Once these three qualities—timeliness, relevance, and accuracy—are in place, the post-event analysis process enables ROI marketers to answer three critical questions:

1. *How well did you do?* The first task in the post-event analysis process is the measurement of results. Data is gathered and fed back into the appropriate analytics, often via execution and PEAT decision support tools. Then, the actual results of individual events are compared to the expected results. The results are aggregated and compared to overall targets as well.

   Measurement alone offers benefits. For one, it enables the company's marketers and leaders to keep a running tally on their progress toward the goals they have set for their spending. It also supports marketing accountability. When targets are tracked through the marketing processes, employees cannot avoid or argue their way out of performance shortfalls. In fact, they are forced to ask another question.

2. *Why did you get those results?* Some marketers measure results and use them to guide future investments but miss the bigger payoffs of post-event analysis because they do not ask why their events produced the results that they did. In fact, the biggest benefits of the post-event analysis process begin to accrue when marketers begin to determine the factors that cause

results. Further, the larger the gap between predicted results and actual results, the larger the opportunity for improvement.

Often, this deeper level of causal analysis requires the assistance of statisticians and other analytical experts, but the payoff in terms of insight is well worth the effort. The reasons behind the gap between expectations and results tell marketers where problems and opportunities are located. It also is a rich source of learning and insight, both of which are needed to power the drive for innovation and improvement, the focus of the third question.

3. *What will you do differently next time?* Once marketers know why their events produce specific results, the next logical step is to put that knowledge to use. Marketers can act on causal knowledge in different ways. They can ignore it and not respond at all, or they can lower their expectations and adjust their analytics. Neither choice is recommended. Rather, the best option is to use this knowledge to improve events by changing the event or by changing the event's cost structure. Successful ROI marketers tend to work both elements to wring the highest levels of improvement possible from the post-event analysis process. Marketers can apply their improvements in any of the four processes. These insights can be used to set more realistic targets and factor in realistic growth projections. They can be used throughout the planning process to adjust investments in brands, geographies, vehicles, and accounts, as well as to change offers. They can be used to create midcourse corrections in the execution process. And when they are used to refine analytics or the suite of output reports, they can improve the post-event analysis process itself. In all of these ways, the marketing process is transformed in a closed loop of learning and continuous improvement.

LG Electronics' Digital Appliances, discussed in Chapter 4, provides an excellent example of the kinds of insights that post-event analysis can yield. As the company delved into the causes of its marketing results across countries, it uncovered a host of opportunities. Many of these were marketing related, such as the discovery that promotions offering gift cards tied to specific retailers were less effective than direct discounts and cash. But others crossed over into other functions. For instance, in one developing nation, the company discovered that design and quality enhancements in their appliances would return significant dividends. LG also discovered that additional investments in retail sales training and point-of-sale displays would generate higher returns in that nation, where the company staffs and runs branded departments within stores owned by other retailers.

POST-EVENT ANALYSIS IN ACTION

Considering marketing results without analysis can easily lead to erroneous and potentially damaging conclusions. The experience of a leading North American wireless service provider, who we'll call Alpha Communications, provides an example.

Alpha Communications was selling its service through three channels. The most promising of these channels was telemarketing, which provided about 13 percent of the company's new customers. It was managed in house and had much higher margins than Alpha's main channel, dealers who demanded higher commissions and required that the company maintain a distribution network. On a cost basis, telemarketing looked like the company's best bet for the future.

In answering the "how did you do" question, however, Alpha discovered that the customers acquired through the telemarketing channel disconnected sooner, and at a significantly higher rate, than those who were

Continued

signed up by dealers. They were, therefore, substantially less profitable. In fact, Alpha calculated the customer period value (CPV)—the net sum of all revenue and costs (including adjustments and bad debt)—associated with each acquisition over a period of 18 months. It discovered that the average CPV for dealers was $296, while for telemarketing it was $166.

The company could have quit there and remained focused on the dealer channel, but instead it asked, "Why did we get that result?" Further analysis revealed the problem: dealers prequalified their customers very carefully and made sure the customer purchased the right plan because their commissions were reduced if the customer discontinued service within three months. The customers reached by telemarketers, on the other hand, were essentially agreeing to whatever rate plan was pitched to them. Then, the first bill arrived and they disconnected, creating bad debt and ill will.

Again, the company could have abandoned the channel, but instead, asked the third question, "What can we do differently?" The answer was to make sure that each prospect was offered a rate plan that he or she could afford. Alpha did that by coding the hundreds of thousands of permutations on the six thousand or so active rate plans in its database at any time. An execution tool was provided to telemarketers that enabled them to help customers chose the right plans. The result: CPV rose, and Alpha was able to focus on telemarketing in order to generate higher overall returns.

When ROI marketers put the third pillar in place, they close the loop on the marketing cycle and supercharge it by integrating analytics and DS tools into their processes. With these three elements in place and aligned, there is just one thing missing—people. In the next chapter and the last pillar, we will examine the issues involved in populating the marketing ROI capability.

Chapter 7

Aligning the Organization around Marketing ROI

Anyone who watched TV in the 1970s will surely remember the boy who hated everything until he tasted Life cereal. The "Mikey" campaign—"He *likes* it! Hey, Mikey!"—was arguably the most popular advertising that the Quaker Oats Company (now a division of PepsiCo) had done for any product since its founding in 1901. The campaign ran for 12 years and, when *TV Guide* ranked the top 50 commercials of all time in 1999, it placed the "Mikey" ad at number 10.

But Mikey, as it turns out, was not all that good at selling cereal.

Dudley Ruch, who is widely regarded as a major influencer in the advancement of quantitative marketing methodology, was Quaker's vice president of marketing research during much of Mikey's run. Over a seven-year period, his department ran analysis after analysis that demonstrated that the ads were *not* helping Quaker sell more Life cereal. Ruch's team did split-tests, market analyses, and statistical modeling; the result was always the same—so was the response from Quaker's management: they liked Mikey, and that was that.

"People are remarkably resistant to facts," reflects Ruch. "They have their theories. They have their truths that they know about how marketing works and, by God, that's how it is, and they are not going to be interested in anything else."

Quaker is not the only company that successfully built its analytical competence but struggled to transform it into a fully developed capacity for marketing ROI. Many companies encounter similar problems. They build analytic engines, provide their employees with decision support tools, and reengineer their marketing processes, and yet nothing changes. Marketing ROI remains an elusive, intangible promise.

When marketing and other employees have access to the analytical insights and tools they need and the path ahead is clearly marked, but the drive to capture profitable volume stalls, it is highly likely that the source of the bottleneck is in the fourth pillar of a marketing ROI system—organizational alignment. This final pillar, which is often neglected but nonetheless critically important, is composed of three essential elements that are required to activate the marketing ROI capability: organizational support, roles and responsibilities, and employee motivation.

Quaker experienced what happens when the first element of the fourth pillar is not in place. Without organizational support, the insights derived from analytics are ignored and business goes on as usual. The support of senior leadership is instrumental here, but don't mistake it for the entire story. Countless change efforts have enjoyed the full commitment of senior leaders and still failed. The advocacy, alignment, and cooperation required to attain this capability must come from a variety of functional, cross-functional, and external sources.

The second element of the organizational alignment pillar is focused on the identification of the roles and responsibilities of all the players. New tools and processes require new ways of working. In order for this new work to become accepted and routinely executed, task assignments and decision rights must be clarified, employee training is required, and an analytical center of excellence containing the specialized skills required in a marketing ROI system must be established.

The third element of the organizational alignment pillar revolves around employee motivation. Again, a company's leadership team can adopt and support a goal, and it can also ensure that everyone has the skills needed to achieve it, but *still* fail to attain it. To avoid this fate, support and skill must be backed up by *will*. Ultimately, the success of marketing ROI depends on the ability of leaders to muster the employee willpower needed to activate the capability. Establishing and reinforcing this organizational willpower requires a combination of intrinsic and extrinsic motivational programs in the form of education, recognition, and rewards.

In short, the three major components of the final pillar provide the answer to the question that in many cases turns out to be the most critical of all: "How do we ensure that people actually do this?"

ORGANIZATIONAL SUPPORT—CONCENTRIC RINGS OF COOPERATION

In the quest to optimize marketing's efforts to differentiate the company's products and services, a marketing ROI system crosses multiple functional boundaries and corporate borders. As these lines are crossed, unexpected barriers to success often arise. Resistance appears as the benefits of this new way of marketing become less and less obvious to those who are being asked to change their behavior. At the same time, aspiring ROI marketers have less power to drive change as they move beyond their formal spheres of influence. They are unable to demand compliance and dependent on voluntary cooperation and support.

In order to develop and maintain the marketing ROI capability, its leaders must first identify all of the areas in which they will need the support of others and then actively enlist that support in each area. In order to accomplish this goal, they need to proactively consider the territorial realities of power as the capability is being planned. A good way to approach this task is in terms of three concentric rings of support encircling the marketing ROI core, as seen in Exhibit 7-1. The first ring encompasses the marketing function itself. The second ring contains the rest of the company—all of the other internal functions the capability affects. The third ring includes all of the organizations outside the company whose assistance is needed to create marketing ROI success, such as media and entertainment companies, retailers and distributors, and information providers.

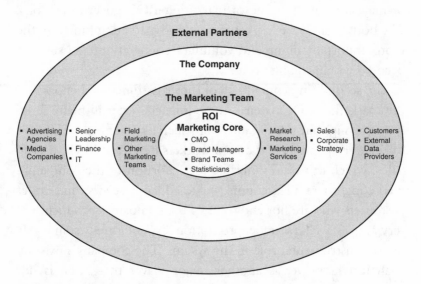

Exhibit 7-1 ROI Concentric Rings of Cooperation

ROI marketers have the greatest degree of power and influence within their own function, but that is not to say that the command-and-control model will suffice when the first ring of support is being developed. In fact, marketing organizations often are remarkably far flung, and the power to lead them can be fragmented among many executives.

In many cases, the marketing function is divided into specialty functions that are not tightly linked. Market research, marketing services (which might produce FSIs—printed advertising inserts—or manage sport sponsorships), brand/product marketing, and field marketing can be separate fiefdoms that must be enlisted in the cause. Further, the marketing function is decentralized in many companies. In these cases, corporate marketers may have little control over operating decisions and events beyond issues relating to the corporate image and brand standards. Or regional or business-based general managers, who may or may not see the value of marketing ROI, govern decisions. The bottom line: the less centralized the marketing function, the more important alignment, voluntary cooperation, and support become within the first ring.

The second ring contains all of the cross-functional impacts of the marketing ROI system. These impacts occur in many functions throughout the organization, such as among the Harrah's call center operators and casino workers described in Chapter 5. Sales, which can be responsible for a portion of the company's marketing to retail accounts, value-added resellers, and other customers who are not end users of the company's products and services, as well as trade promotion expenditures, commonly play an instrumental role in the system. The company's existing analytical firepower is another major player that often is not located within the marketing function. Finance will be called upon to provide data and validate ROI investment, methodologies, and analyses. R&D may be asked to redesign products based on customer preferences revealed by the analytics. Manufacturing and logistics may need to adjust production and inventory levels or help reengineer products so that they can be profitably marketed. The willingness and effectiveness with which all of these functions respond will have an effect on marketing ROI results.

In the third and outermost ring are external partners. As discussed in Chapter 4, certain types of data required to fuel analytics come from external sources such as marketing service providers and channel partners. Also, the insights revealed by marketing ROI will stimulate changes in event execution as well as vehicle investment levels. Thus, companies may want to buy media differently or change the structure of existing sponsorships or alter the terms and conditions of retail promotions. The alignment and cooperation of external partners can be critical to the success of all of these efforts.

So how can aspiring ROI marketers ensure that all of these parties are properly enlisted in the effort to grow profitable volume?

The CEO and the company's senior leadership team play a major role in this task. As always, it is the responsibility of senior leaders to ensure that the organization is aligned with and held accountable for the accomplishment of any major initiative. These senior executives have the power to eliminate cross-functional barriers if and when they arise. In fact, unless top management values ROI metrics, demands accountability, and helps resolve disagreements, the odds of developing marketing ROI as an organizational capability are nil.

One effective means of enlisting the support of senior leadership is by emphasizing the tangible returns of marketing ROI.

It is a rare executive who won't give a fair hearing to a business case that is built on profitability. "We suffer as marketers when people think we're just giving them jive talk," says Beth Comstock, GE's CMO. "People really listen when you have money on the table, when you have a real action plan."

Another effective means of enlisting senior leadership support is by becoming a model of ROI accountability. Marketing ROI thrives in fact-based cultures of accountability, and several members of the ANA taskforce on marketing accountability went so far as to suggest that "no amount of analytical artifice would succeed" unless such a culture exists.[1] Whether or not this is always true, a marketing leader's commitment and behavior is crucial to maintaining the network of leadership support needed to activate the capability. As American Express CMO John Hayes said about earning the confidence of senior management, "What is most important, though, is having clear measurements for all initiatives and ensuring that the organization sees the CMO hold himself or herself accountable for all marketplace results."

Of course, the support of senior leadership is only one piece of the organizational alignment pillar. Marketing ROI success also requires that processes be staffed with competent people, that these people have the skills required to execute the processes, and that they are willing to undertake the work.

DEFINING ROLES AND RESPONSIBILITIES

Marketing ROI systems create fundamental changes in the way that a company conducts its marketing and sales. As the everyday business of marketing changes, new ways of thinking and working are required from everyone involved in the analytical marketing effort—from the top down. This, in turn, creates the need for new job descriptions, employee training programs, and hiring profiles. Further, a center of excellence to house the analytical expertise is needed. This center must be staffed by people with specialized skills, who can create, maintain, and analyze the results of the insight engines that drive marketing ROI.

Preparing to Lead

Usually, a business unit leader or the CMO (or the company's senior marketer, whatever the title) is the leader of the marketing ROI effort. The best choice for this leadership role is someone who is responsible for the entire marketing organization and also serves as a member of the company's senior leadership team.

The role of leader comes with responsibilities. It requires a thorough understanding of each of the components in all four pillars. These leaders must be able to ask the right questions, evaluate analytical proposals, and judge the progress of the effort. Generally, this is not a major problem for the average business unit leader or CMO. Most of them already understand the mechanics of process building and the issues that arise in organizational change (the third and fourth pillars). The decision support tools of the second pillar are also fairly easy to evaluate. Most executives have worked their way up the ladder and so have a solid understanding of their current work processes, the information available to them, and how to accomplish the job. They also need to know how to use data, metrics, and reports to track performance. This knowledge enables them to judge whether brand and field marketers will find a tool easy and intuitive to use. In all three pillars, however, the initiative's leader must be willing to make the time to deal with the issues involved in the pillars at a detailed level.

The analytical knowledge required to lead a marketing ROI effort is more problematic. Leaders don't need PhDs in statistics, but they do need to understand how models or other analytical techniques work, and when and where they are best applied. Initiative leaders use this knowledge to act as quality control managers. It enables them to ensure that marketing's newfound analytical prowess is producing the right insights, knowledge, and actions. This is combined with a detailed understanding of the above to ensure that the developmental plan is correct and that the pillars are coming together as they should. As important, leaders of marketing ROI must be able to judge the competence of the specialists they will hire and depend on to build the pillars.

Sometimes initiative leaders are able to obtain a portion of this knowledge within their companies. Training in other types of business analytics, such as statistical process control, activity-based costing, and balanced scorecards, can provide a foundation for understanding marketing ROI. "The analytical is something I've had to learn," Beth Comstock told us. "And thank goodness for my GE experience. No matter what your line of work is in GE, you're put through Six Sigma–type training that really teaches you analytics. . . . I don't think I would have gotten that had I just stayed within the media world."

Continuing education programs offer another viable path to this knowledge. Most major business schools are offering courses in marketing analytics. Professional organizations such as the Association of National Advertisers, which hosts peer forums and task forces, are also a rich source of knowledge. Formal and informal benchmarking with noncompetitors is another good way to learn the nuances of analytical marketing. Witness the connections that GE CEO Jeffrey Immelt established with leaders from P&G and Johnson & Johnson when he decided that GE needed a more robust marketing orientation. Finally, marketing ROI leaders can utilize expert advisors in lieu of developing personal analytical competence. (The problem with this route is judging who is competent and whose advice can be trusted. If you choose this approach, we suggest that you use several independent experts and "triangulate" their advice, particularly as it relates to the soundness of statistical analysis or other highly technical issues that you might encounter as you build a full capability.)

New Job Definitions, Training, and Hiring Profiles

New tools and processes create changes in the roles and responsibilities of the employees who use them. New skills are needed, and this creates impacts on the jobs, training, and hiring of marketers and other employees involved in marketing ROI.

The most obvious impact that this shift has on employees is in how they execute their jobs on a day-to-day basis. Sometimes employees have entirely new roles to play in processes that did not exist previously. Sometimes their jobs are altered only slightly. In any case, as the marketing ROI effort moves forward and the capability evolves, the new roles and responsibilities of employees need to be clarified and defined in detail.

The most direct way to approach this work is by mapping and then, tracing the four new processes created in the third pillar. For each, answer basic questions about the flow of work, like these:

- Who will oversee each process?
- Who will execute each step in the process?
- What decisions need to be made?

- Who will be responsible for inputs into decisions, and who will have final say?
- What new skills will the process workers require to do their jobs?

When these questions are answered, employees must be prepared to assume their new roles. Training is a critical issue in a marketing ROI system (indeed, in the development of any capability) that is not always fully appreciated. In our experience, successful training programs require three elements: concentrated time, that is, dedicated sessions in which the trainees are not distracted by the demands of their everyday responsibilities; real-world tasks, that is, the training's outcomes should be something they will use on the job, such as next year's plan; and expert trainers, who not only know every nuance of the subject but also make the time to work one on one with the trainees to ensure outcomes.

Successful ROI marketers work hard to ensure that their employees have the training they need to use analytical tools and execute ROI-based processes. Some of these companies, such as P&G, are well known for their emphasis on the internal development of their marketers. "If you're not training—especially at a company that's promoting from within—you can't expect to grow," says Jim Stengel, P&G's global marketing officer. "We need to be outstanding trainers and never be complacent about that."

GE is another company that has emphasized training as an enabler of analytical marketing. In 2004, under the leadership of Beth Comstock, GE identified training needs around nine sales and marketing skill sets, including analytical and market research techniques. The company then partnered with Northwestern's Kellogg School of Management and the University of Michigan to create training modules for GE's business units and marketing professionals.

Finally, the shift to analytic marketing also creates change in the hiring profiles for marketers. Traditionally, creativity and intuition were the primary qualities of a viable marketing candidate. Today, analytical skills are an equally important part of the mix.

Says Diageo's senior marketer Rob Malcolm: "Having keen analytical skills and capability is a foundation that all marketers must have. Whether you were a mathematics major or not, the ability to penetrate both hard and soft data—to synthesize and draw meaning, conclusions, and priorities—is an essential foundation. In marketing, you need to use both halves of your brain. You need to have the analytics. You also need to have the intuition. And you have to be quite flexible at using and leveraging both parts of your brain. There's a lot of talk now about 'whole-brain' marketers."

Of course, hiring a company full of whole-brain marketers, each of whom possesses the ideal mix of creative and analytical skills, is very difficult. The application of analytics to marketing is still relatively early in its development, and many marketers simply have not developed these skills as yet. Further, marketers who do have those skills are in high demand and thus a challenge to locate, hire, and retain. For these reasons, it may be more practical to think in terms of the overall balance of the marketing team. Instead of struggling to find individuals with all of the right skills, hire the candidates with the highest levels of specific skills and use them to build a balanced team that has the right mix of creative and analytic skills as a whole.

A Center of Excellence

The final set of roles and responsibilities that must be defined in the fourth pillar are focused on the development of a center of excellence (COE). This COE is the headquarters of the specialized analytical expertise that marketing ROI requires.

Typically, a COE is staffed with the statisticians and research specialists who understand and recommend data and analytical approaches. These are the people who build and maintain the models as well as the algorithms that power them. They make sure the DS tools and processes on which marketing ROI depends are in good working order and that employees are using them properly. In addition, they help the company's marketers set up research and deconstruct analytical results—determining the causes of performance shortfalls and using them to refine the company's analytic engines and improve future results.

The development of a marketing ROI capability demands an internal COE. Parts of this specialized expertise can be outsourced, but, by definition, an organizational capability is something that is owned, not rented.

The size of the COE is entirely dependent on the size of the company's commitment to analytics and marketing ROI. Capital One, whose entire business model is built around analytics, has over 100 statisticians on staff. These specialists partner with ad hoc cross-functional teams to create and test new solutions. A midsized company that utilizes analytics solely for marketing may employ just one or two statisticians, who supervise outside experts who are hired on a project basis.

While the typical COE is staffed with people who are more familiar with advanced mathematics than marketing, they usually have a leader who is conversant in both worlds. This individual needs a depth and breadth of analytical expertise, as well as a clear understanding of how analytics can be applied to the business. When a new media vehicle appears, this is the person who will determine what data and analytical approach will be needed to measure its results. Rich Mirman, who was one of the first people that Gary Loveman hired after accepting the COO position at Harrah's, is a good example of such a manager. Mirman received his bachelor of science degree in mathematics from the University of Wisconsin–Madison and a master's in mathematics from the State University of New York–Stony Brook. He was also a graduate student of economics at the University of Chicago before working with our firm and designing marketing analytics for various clients. After joining Harrah's as vice president of relationship marketing, he helped the gaming company build what has since become well known as a leading analytical COE.

If marketing is the COE's primary "customer," it makes sense that the COE should be located within the marketing function. This is where the marketing effectiveness group is situated in P&G, for example. But COEs can be and often are located in different functions within their companies. What is more important than location is that the COE is expert and independent. The COE imposes requirements and conditions regarding data, analytics, and DS tools. It is a guardian of the truth, so it must be frank and forthcoming about marketing failures as well as successes. Because it must, it is essential that the COE be unbiased in its findings; likewise, it must be led by an independent, intelligent person of high integrity.

For these reasons there is a natural tension between the COE and the rest of the marketing organization. That is another reason why the COE's role in helping marketers analyze and optimize their results is so important. In doing so, these specialists come to be viewed as the solution to marketers' problems, not problems in and of themselves.

MOTIVATING ROI MARKETERS

The successful development and utilization of the marketing ROI capability ultimately rests in the hands of employees. When companies launch these initiatives, roughly one-quarter of the people involved enthusiastically accept and adopt the mindset and behavioral changes that are required. But the reaction of the other three-quarters ranges from conditional support to wary neutrality to outright resistance. The third major element of the organizational alignment pillar is aimed at ensuring that as many people in the latter group come to accept and support the effort.

Ignoring or underestimating this prerequisite can endanger all of the work that has gone before. As the ANA task force noted: "Marketers must WANT to be measured, must embrace accountability or even the most artfully designed metrics will ultimately fail."[2] But how do you get employees to *want* to practice ROI marketing? The twofold answer: encourage and nurture intrinsic motivation, and support it with informal and formal extrinsic incentives.

The most powerful energy that marketing ROI leaders can harness in their quest for profitable volume is the personal motivation of employees. But this motivation—the force that compels people to act—cannot be imposed by corporate or managerial edict. It is voluntarily generated with each individual employee. Happily, there are compelling intrinsic motivators inherent in marketing ROI that its leaders can articulate to help this process along:

- *It enhances the professionalism of marketers, in the pure sense of the word.* It should be an intrinsic motivator that is a worthy objective in and of itself. ROI marketers know what does and doesn't work. This enables them to improve their performance and practice their craft at the most competent levels.

- *Marketing ROI is empowering in the corporate sense.* It enhances the marketer's position within the company. The ability to measure marketing results and specify returns enables marketers to assert a greater degree of control over budgets and gain a voice in decision making, especially in industries and companies in which the profession is still marginalized.
- *Analytics are an integral piece of the future of marketing.* It has become clear that analytical marketing will be an essential skill set for tomorrow's marketing professional. Thus, the opportunity to participate in marketing ROI is a valuable experience that adds a key skill to the marketer's tool kit, a skill that will pay dividends over and over through one's career.

In short, when marketers undertake this work, they become more valuable to their companies, they become more successful in their jobs, and their career satisfaction is enhanced.

Marketing ROI leaders can and should talk about what they want to do and why, and make compelling business and personal cases for change. But the intrinsic motivation required to sustain these efforts must be supported by informal and formal extrinsic incentives, too. Informal incentives, such as praise for a job well done, recognition as a future leader of the company, and other rewards, help create converts and initiative momentum. Formal incentives, usually delivered in the form of redesigned compensation systems, put employees on notice that the company is serious about marketing ROI and give teeth to initiatives. When employees see that their paychecks are involved, they understand that management is intent on change, and they pay close attention.

Of course, there is always a small percentage of employees who cannot be influenced by formal or informal incentives. Some of them will be incapable of adapting to a marketing ROI mindset, and their managers will have to be prepared to replace them with more capable employees. Some of them will simply refuse to change or actively resist change. In those cases, managers will have to act publicly and with authority to ensure that the success of a marketing ROI effort is not jeopardized.

There are three basic components in an effective marketing ROI incentive system, as shown in Exhibit 7-2: volume, profit, and qualitative performance objectives. The system must also be accurately measured and tied to individual achievement.

A marketing ROI incentive system must be based in large part on the degree to which employees can generate profitable volume—not just in the corporate sense, but profitability and

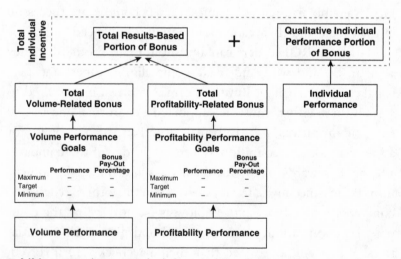

Exhibit 7-2 Volume, Profitability, and Qualitative Objectives That Determine Incentives

volume that is linked to the direct effort of individual employees. (Generally speaking, the compensation of marketing and sales-people has not been based on their volume and profit consistently.) In such a system, the volume and ROI targets for advertising and promotion spending are set simultaneously in a formal annual plan, and are balanced with and dependent upon each other. Thus, if a manager can raise the effectiveness of his or her spending, he or she should automatically get the benefit of additional volume and profits, too. Further, volume and ROI need to be tracked on an organizational and individual level and, in turn, these results become the primary basis for incentive bonuses.

Incentive systems should also take marketing's qualitative targets into account. These might include brand-building goals such as increasing net promoter scores or the lifetime value of customers. Usually, these qualitative targets are assigned a smaller part of incentive pool and change as brand objectives shift.

The compensation model in Exhibit 7-2 offers a high degree of flexibility. Assuming that employees will move toward the goals that increase their compensation, changes in the overall weighting between volume and profitability, as well as shifts in qualitative performance targets, can be used to drive employee behavior. By altering the payout percentages for goals, "conditional" weighting plans can be created and balanced results encouraged. (If, for instance, the target payout percentages for volume and profitability are both set at a high level, but the payout percentages drop after the target is reached, employees will work toward reaching both target goals rather than favoring one side of the compensation plan.) And, depending on the company's objectives, payouts can be capped or unlimited, which further influences employee behavior.

One major consideration in this system is the relative weighting among profitability, volume performance, and other qualitative targets. The more weight that is assigned to profitability, the more incentive there is for employees to focus their efforts in that direction. (Of course, volume still remains an important part of the mix; an exaggerated emphasis on profitability can hurt brands.) Companies need to customize their incentive programs to meet their specific circumstances and the function of the employees participating in the plan. In the case of marketers, for instance, profitability and volume are often assigned equal weighting, typically 35 percent to 45 percent each, and the remaining 10 percent to 30 percent is assigned to the qualitative targets on which the company is currently focused.

Employee compensation plans should not be changed arbitrarily. If a company is going to link compensation to ROI, it also must be able to measure ROI accurately, and the plan must be equitable. To ensure this outcome, "soft" launches for marketing ROI incentive plans are often used.

The initial phase of such a launch often involves no change at all. Instead, employees are given the opportunity to learn and use the capability through several marketing cycles. This process often takes place during a pilot stage in the marketing ROI program, when the focus is on learning and performing new tasks, and informal incentives can be very motivating. They are also informed that on a set date in the near future their compensation will be linked to the capability. Then, targets are set, but are not linked to compensation for several more cycles. In this way, employees get the chance to see how the plan will work and, if necessary, improve their skills before it has a negative impact on their paychecks. Only then, after the specified period, the new plan becomes fully operative.

Finally, redesigned incentive systems are individualized. In other words, they must feature a direct link to the individual employee's performance. This may be a partial link; in fact, some percentage of compensation should be tied to overall corporate, business unit, and/or team performance. But it is also important that personal objectives are included and the employee's effort actually influences her rewards. At Diageo, for instance, the compensation of global brand managers is directly linked to the results associated with their individual brands. "One of my first actions was to tie the bonuses of my global brand directors to business performance," says Rob Malcolm. "A significant part of my global brand directors' bonuses is tied directly to the top- *and* bottom-line performance of their specific business."

* * * *

With the final pillar in place, the major components of the marketing ROI capability are complete and fully integrated. But knowing what a capability should look like and how it works is not the same as actually managing its development. In the next and final chapter, we will offer six principles to guide you as your company embarks on the quest for profitable volume. And we show how the Kellogg Company, the largest maker of breakfast cereals in the United States, used them to successfully manage its first marketing ROI initiative.

Chapter 8

Undertaking the Marketing ROI Transformation

he preceding chapters comprise a high-level road map to developing an organizational capability for profit-driven marketing. This final chapter describes how aspiring ROI marketers can customize this road map and ensure that their initiatives get off to a successful start.

There are several reasons why the route to marketing ROI must be customized. For one, every company's marketing landscape is unique, and typically a high-level road map cannot reflect every aspect of that reality. Every industry operates within a different marketing environment. Thus, the offers and vehicles that can be effectively deployed by companies within the consumer-driven CPG sector, for instance, are quite different from those used in the business-to-business environment of the enterprise software sector. Further, every company has a unique marketing strategy. Both Apple and Dell sell personal computers, but their positioning, strategy, and go-to-market channels are distinct and require different offers and vehicles. In much the same way, your road map to marketing ROI must chart a unique route that has been plotted specifically for your business.

Another reason why generic road maps require customization is that every company occupies a different starting point on the ever-expanding marketing ROI continuum. As we've seen, a few companies have been developing this capability for decades.

In other companies, the ability to measure and predict consumer response accurately will seem more like science fiction than science. And the rest of the companies in the corporate universe are starting somewhere between the two extremes. We can ink a theoretical x onto a map and declare it the starting point of marketing ROI. But in reality, you must start from wherever *you* are.

Finally, because marketing ROI is a capability, you must always be ready and willing to revise your road map in order to reach new and more desirable end points. The rationale and basic structure of the pillars that support this capability should be relatively stable over time, but the knowledge, skills, and technology are always improving to enable companies to compete in an ever-changing environment. For instance, the emergence of a new media vehicle can create a wave of change throughout the marketing function. Often, it will dictate a new data stream and require a new analytical approach to ROI measurement. Transforming the output of this new approach into actionable knowledge may require a new decision support tool that field marketers must be trained to use. Thus, your road map needs to take into account the fact that sometimes the level of marketing ROI capability you need to build will be a moving target.

THE PRINCIPLES OF MARKETING ROI TRANSFORMATION

Once you have customized your road map and are ready to undertake the journey required to develop the marketing ROI capability, the ability to adapt to and successfully undertake change will become even more important. The development journey is rarely a linear process. Even when the leadership team has established a master plan, the sequencing of your initiatives will be influenced by corporate priorities and budgets and all the other variables that effect business change efforts.

In addition, the four pillars usually are erected concurrently, not serially. Because the ROI marketer's first question is always, "What can I do to sell something today?" you should not invest all of your resources and time in a long-term effort to build a comprehensive repertoire of analytic approaches that, theoretically at least, will all be in place on a set date and magically confer the benefits of a full marketing ROI capability. Instead, it is far more practical to examine your marketing spend and begin improving the effectiveness of its largest and most important component immediately. So, develop the analytical approach that best addresses this major spending component, along with the decision support tools, process changes, and training it requires, and put them to work to enhance profitability as quickly as possible. Then begin to expand your marketing ROI capacity to the other marketing cost "buckets" in descending order.

Finally, here are a set of transformation principles derived from successful marketing ROI initiatives. These six principles will help you improve the odds of implementation success:

1. *Align with the corporate value-creation strategy for customers and consumers.* The development of this capability does not occur in a vacuum. Accordingly, it has a greater chance of attracting support and succeeding when it is tightly aligned with the existing value focus (which might be innovation, customer service, quality and excellence, global reach, or something else) within the company.

2. *Establish vision.* Marketing ROI initiatives require a vision that is ambitious, rewarding, and compelling in order to gain the levels of employee commitment and managerial support they

need to succeed. This vision must be broadly and repeatedly disseminated.

3. *Create champions.* Sound strategy and effective tactics are important elements in the success of these initiatives, but people turn the wheels of change. These initiatives require champions who are passionate about the vision, will commit their own time and resources to bringing it to life, and are capable of recruiting others to the cause. Champions are needed at the beginning of the initiative, and as the initiative expands at each new level of employee participation it touches.

4. *Pilot early.* Pilot projects serve a variety of useful purposes in launching marketing ROI efforts. Most importantly, they enable you to figure out what is wrong (and something surely will be) with your plans and designs *before* you drive for scale. Thus, they surface false assumptions and other problems before major investments are made, as well as enable fast and efficient starts, and create learning opportunities and insights as to the best path forward, as well as a new cadre of champions.

5. *Demonstrate success.* Words alone are not enough to convince others to commit the substantial amounts of resources and time needed for these initiatives. By demonstrating even a relatively small portion of the success the initiative is expected to produce, it is much easier to convince others to join the effort and stay with it through the inevitable discouraging moments.

6. *Maintain momentum and solidify gains.* Maintaining the momentum of marketing ROI initiatives requires thought and effort. You must be prepared to address the resistance and often unexpected obstacles that arise when traditional work

practices, cultural mores, and departmental prerogatives are challenged. You also must be prepared to identify and pursue the initiative that will provide the next success and solidify the gains that have been made.

The best way to understand how these principles work together to facilitate the successful development of the marketing ROI capability is to see how they have been applied in the real world. Toward that end, let's examine how Kellogg Company, the $11.8 billion breakfast and snack behemoth, quietly and radically transformed its pricing and promotion spending on ready-to-eat cereals.[1]

THE ROI OF BREAKFAST CEREAL

Walking down the cereal aisle at the local grocery store and perusing the colorful cartoon characters, celebrity spokespeople, and tie-ins with Hollywood blockbusters found on cereal boxes, it is easy to get the impression that ready-to-eat cereal is a fun business. But in reality, the aisle is the frontline in a pitched battle that is being waged in a hotly contested market worth $7.75 billion annually in the United States alone. Since 2002, Kellogg has been holding its own in the cereal wars. In 2007, the company's centennial year, it laid claim to 30 percent of the domestic market, selling $2.8 billion worth of cereal in North America, and another $3.3 billion worth internationally.

It should come as no surprise that Kellogg supports its leading position with lots of marketing: in 2007, it reported that its total consumer and trade promotion expenditures approached 30 percent of revenue. In fact, the company has been one of the world's great marketing organizations since the day that

William Keith (W. K.) Kellogg formed the Battle Creek Toasted Corn Flake Co.

W. K. was a marketing zealot in an era when few manufacturers had gotten the call. In those early days, he wrote his own copy and boasted that he spent as much on promoting and advertising his products as he did on dividends for his shareholders. W. K. realized how important it was to get as much product as possible into grocery stores. During his first year, he spent a third of his working capital to place a full-page advertisement in *Ladies' Home Journal* that asked women to pester their grocers to carry Kellogg's Corn Flakes. A year later, he suggested that the ladies wink at their favorite cereal purveyors on Wednesdays. Those who did were rewarded with a sample box of Kellogg's Corn Flakes. As time went on, and the counters of the dry goods merchant gave way to the aisles of the modern supermarket, gaining shelf space became an even more critical and costly component of the company's marketing spend.

By the 1990s, trade promotion had become an expense that most cereal marketers thought of as a necessary evil. "We referred to 'buy one, get one free' as a drug that you couldn't get off," says Tom Knowlton, president of Kellogg USA from 1994 to 1998 (who went on to serve as the dean of the faculty of business at Ryerson University).

Kellogg's trade promotions pumped up sales in the short term, but they also had a dark side. Take Kellogg's All-Bran cereal, for example. Over the course of eight decades, Kellogg had nurtured All-Bran's positioning as a healthy product rich in dietary fiber, and its devotees were willing to pay a premium for it. But as consumers learned that the next two-for-one deal was always just around the corner, they would wait to buy All-Bran. Sometimes while they waited, they would begin eating a cheaper store brand. In addition, every dollar that Kellogg spent on trade promotions was a dollar that could not be spent burnishing All-Bran's image.

At that time, trade promotions tended to emphasize volume over profitability, and so were also squeezing the company's cereal margins. The performance of salespeople was measured by the pound-share of their accounts, and as a number of Kellogg's sales reps told us, if they were behind plan, they'd sell a truckload of Kellogg's Raisin Bran simply because it was heavier than other cereals. Shudders still run up and down Knowlton's spine when he thinks about the flurry of year-end promotional deals that the Kellogg's sales force made to meet its volume quotas. "I remember we would finish a calendar year and wouldn't find out until two or three months later that we had had a negative pull through of $20 or $30 million," he recalls.

These losses were caused by a practice known as "forward buying," in which retailers and wholesalers buy more discounted product than they need for a promotional event and resell it later or in other outlets at full price. "The customer would buy in at the low price and sell it at the high, so we weren't getting any return," explains Dale Lazarro, a Kellogg's account manager assigned to an independent grocery store chain at the time.

So it came to be that in the spring of 1998, Sue Karibjanian, Kellogg's former senior vice president of sales, stood before the company's board and asked for $21 million to resolve the trade promotion conundrum once and for all. She told the board that the money was a drop in the bucket compared with the $600 million that Kellogg's was spending on thousands of trade promotion events annually. And then she showed the board several charts illustrating the results of an analysis of the company's trade promotion events.

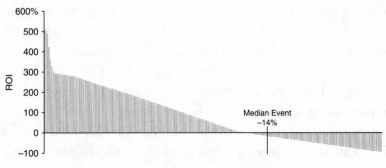

Source: Event history database

Exhibit 8-1 Kellogg's Trade Promotion ROI by Event

Exhibit 8-1 showed that most of Kellogg's trade promotion events—59 percent, in fact—lost money for the company. Exhibit 8-2 showed that the profit generated by the other 41 percent of events was almost entirely chewed up by those events that lost money. Overall, the average (mean) of Kellogg's trade

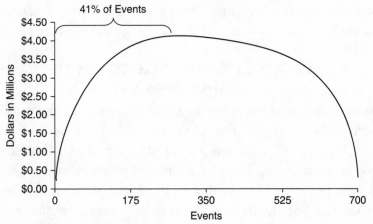

Source: Event history database

Exhibit 8-2 Kellogg's Cumulative Event Contribution

promotion ROI was a dismal 5 percent and the median event was 14 percent "We also had a chart that showed where the money was going," says Karibjanian. "The numbers of accounts that had a negative ROI was shocking."

It didn't have to be this way, Karibjanian told the board. The return on trade dollars could be significantly improved by allocating the funds differently. She said that the $21 million would be spent to continue to develop and roll out custom software that would enable sales reps across the company to select and structure promotional events for optimal ROI. She said that the company would save $65 million annually by eliminating trade promotion inefficiencies *and* increase volume at the same time.

Even if the fine points of trade promotion spending washed over the directors, who included Carly Fiorina, who was at the time with Lucent, and Donald Rumsfeld, then with Gilead Sciences, they knew a good deal when they heard one. Karibjanian got the money, and with it Kellogg's Trade Promotion Excellence (TPE) initiative gained the funding it needed to become an integral component of the company's sales and marketing functions.

ALIGNING TPE WITH KELLOGG'S VALUE CREATION STRATEGY

Many large-scale change initiatives fail because they aren't firmly anchored in the larger goals of the organization. From its inception, however, TPE was directly linked to both the challenges the company was facing in the marketplace, which included a slow, but prolonged decline in market share and prices, as well as a broader and deeper strategic effort to transform to a value-based management system that was sweeping through the company headquarters in Battle Creek at the time.

In the mid-1990s, the ready-to-eat cereal industry was in the doldrums. A Salomon Brothers analysis published in that era summed up the state of the cereal market:

In the late 1980s to early 1990s, pricing and volumes were plentiful, with heavy promotional spends being paid for by semi-annual price increases of 6–7%. However, as we progressed through the 1990s, the heavy pricing, heavy volume gains that we saw ended in a consumer backlash to high prices and a decrease in volume due to just-in-time inventory. With the decrease in volumes came the deceleration of inefficient promotional spending, such as buy one, get one free (BOGOs).

With the reduction in promotional spending, category growth came to a halt. In 1995, it grew 0.5% in all channels, and approximately 1.5% in 1996 (year to date [1997], the category is up 1%). These figures are far below the 3.5% historical category growth trend and below the 2.8% growth trend since 1992.

As a result of the decrease in volumes and the threat of private label, cereal manufacturers began cutting prices on cereals in order to stimulate growth—in fact, we have been in an era of price deflation since 1994.[2]

Kellogg's was facing its most difficult challenges since the end of World War I, when shortages of raw materials and rail cars forced the company to cancel its advertising and sampling program and borrow heavily to meet operating expenses. By 1994, its market share in the United States had been slowly but steadily declining for 20 years, from about 43 percent to 33 percent. Net sales had continued to rise, as they had every year since 1934, but only modestly—7 percent in 1992, 2 percent in 1993, and 4 percent in 1994.

This was the environment that Tom Knowlton inherited when he was named president of Kellogg USA, but he thought he had a solution to the challenge. As head of the company's cereal business in Canada and the United Kingdom, Knowlton had tested a concept known as Value-Based Management (VBM). VBM called for a shift away from revenue-based measures of performance, such as net income, to value-based metrics, such as profitability. (Today, the company characterizes this as a shift from "volume to value.") Eager to revamp Kellogg USA in accordance with VBM principles, Knowlton set up a task force consisting of his direct reports and top executives at Kellogg's two advertising agencies, Leo Burnett and J. Walter Thompson. The group met for two or three days every month from October 1994 to May 1995, first looking back at how the company had gotten to where it was and then preparing a vision for the future, christened "Snapshot 2000." In July 1995, the board of directors gave its blessing to this five-year plan that called for Kellogg's to hold its prices by building internal efficiencies in its new product development, supply chain, and manufacturing processes, and gradually shift back to building brands rather than propping them up with profligate trade spend. "It completely changed the metrics we were using from volume and market share at all costs to economic profit," Knowlton recalls. "It was a major transition and transformation for the management and the company."

Holding the line on prices, however, became impossible in 1996, as Kraft Foods slashed prices on its Post cereals by an average of 20 percent and General Mills continued its aggressive trade promotions. Alan Harris, then Kellogg USA's marketing chief, convened another task force to formulate a response, which recommended that the company cut prices and promotional spending on about two-thirds of its brands (those considered more commoditylike) by an average of 12 percent.

The inception of the TPE initiative was rooted in these market pressures, as well as the needs and goals they spawned. Management was already focused on developing *profitable* volume, and the company could neither afford to lose more market share nor cut its margins still further to maintain it. The time was right to address the optimization of Kellogg's trade spending. And so in late 1996, approximately 18 months before Sue Karibjanian stood before the board and asked for a major financial commitment, Harris asked Dan Doore, a strategic analyst reporting directly to Kellogg's North American CFO, to create a team to take on the trade promotion challenge.

ESTABLISHING A COMPELLING VISION FOR TPE

Before Doore and his team could formulate a vision for TPE that Kellogg's management and employees would feel compelled to buy into, they had to understand what was and was not working in the company's trade promotions. This was problematic because, at that time, Kellogg's was not calculating ROI at the promoted group level (i.e., a group of stock-keeping units promoted together), the level at which salespeople made decisions. Thus, in order to learn how much incremental profitability and volume Kellogg's was earning when it promoted a particular brand or size, the TPE team created and analyzed a historical database covering nearly 700 events for 26 SKUs across 33 accounts from the fourth quarter of 1996.

This database was built from external volume and merchandising data purchased from Information Resources, Inc. (IRI) along with internal event cost, shipment, base price, and free-standing-insert circulation data. The TPE team used it to match spending to events and shipments to consumption, as well as to calculate the retail trade margins. The results were eye opening.

The team discovered that much of the conventional wisdom about promotions was not so wise. For instance, the analytics revealed that the $1.99 or lower price point that Kellogg's marketers had heretofore believed was necessary to drive promotion sales was a myth. In fact, the display mattered more than the price point. When the number of displays are equal, the product could be promoted at $2.99 and deliver the same amount of lift and significantly more profit than when promoted at $1.99. The team also discovered that promotions did not cause significant cannibalization within a brand. In other words, the gains earned by promoting 20-ounce Frosted Flakes were not being negated by lost sales on the 15-ounce box. Seasonality, however, did matter. Although many brands did not fare well when they were promoted in December, Rice Krispies' lift, perhaps because the cereal was used in variety of homemade holiday snacks, was phenomenal. Promotions on Special K, on the other hand, did poorly in December, but delivered great lift in January, when consumers' New Year's diet resolutions were still fresh in their minds.

Of course, the most discouraging findings, as Sue Karibjanian would soon inform the board, were that 59 percent of the events studied had lost money and that the net ROI was a paltry 5 percent. The scatter chart in Exhibit 8-3, which shows that Kellogg's lost money on the majority of its promotions while retailers almost always made money, was a particularly grim portrait of the situation. Doore describes the chart as a "stark, fact-based picture of something that was an incredibly broken mess."

These findings and a simultaneous review of the company's trade promotion processes built the business case for a vision of TPE that was driven by three goals: profitable volume, sales rep empowerment, and the exploitation of variation. They were defined as follows:

- *Profitable volume.* Treat promotion-funding dollars as a scarce resource and invest them in the areas where they will yield the

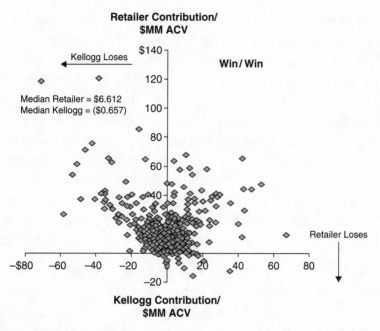

Exhibit 8-3 The Kellogg-Retailer Contribution Imbalance

highest return. A focus on volume—while maintaining the retailers' margins—all too often leads to a manufacturer's loss. Events should be selected and structured to optimize profit for both parties, and Kellogg's should demand better quality of performance from the retailers. It may seem like common sense, but in consumer products marketing, seeking volume and assuming profit would follow had historically been the rule.

- *Sales rep empowerment.* Events should be tailored to the needs of the specific account and selected by each sales rep, within certain guidelines, rather than being predetermined by a national calendar composed, in command-and-control fashion, in Battle Creek. Improved analytic and decisions support tools will be necessary to enable reps to choose among many options to make the best decisions for their accounts, to negotiate from stronger positions, and to assure consistent quality across accounts. Since sales reps will be developing as well as executing promotion plans, they should be rewarded for volume and profit results, not just for mindless execution.

- *Exploitation of variation.* All brands are not created equal; nor are all accounts; nor are all events. Exploit the positive and eliminate the negative. Simplistically, this means stop funding unprofitable accounts and start funding good ones. Stop supporting unprofitable brands and start supporting good ones. Stop buying bad events and buy more good ones.

In summary, the TPE team's vision was to empower the sales force with the proper tools and authority and hold it accountable for attaining profitable volume by taking advantage of the strengths of particular brands, events, and accounts. With it, the team clearly articulated the initiative's purpose and described how it planned to optimize trade promotion spending. As Doore says, "You can't over-communicate about the vision, making sure that the process, tools and implementation are always leading back to that vision."

CREATING TPE CHAMPIONS

The third principle of marketing ROI transformation, and perhaps the most critical, is the need for champions. These champions are the architects of the capability; certainly that was the case with Kellogg's TPE initiative. As Dan Doore told us, "Big change involves a lot of people. You'll get there together, or you just won't get there."

Kellogg's culture has always bred smart, devoted managers, and that's another major reason why TPE successfully took root there. TPE enjoyed the support of champions such as senior leaders Tom Knowlton and Alan Harris, who pushed for change. Dan Doore was a champion who was fearless about taking on sacred but false truths and who kept the project on an even keel. Sue Karibjanian championed TPE with the board, as well as being a vocal supporter who challenged the TPE team to train her staff appropriately; in turn, she challenged her staff to do their homework. But in our opinion, one of TPE's most influential champions was Phil Straniero, who was truly the right person in the right place at the right time.

When the TPE initiative was born, Straniero had a quarter-century of selling for Kellogg's under his belt. He started as a sales rep in southeast Indiana in 1971 and rose, like so many Kellogg's executives, through the ranks. He served as a district manager, a major account manager, an assistant division sales manager, and a division sales manager. While running the sunny Southern California and Las Vegas region in the 1980s, Straniero's market share rose from 33 to 42 percent over five years. "The president of the company at the time nicknamed me 'Lucky,'" says Straniero.

Soon Straniero was summoned from "paradise" to return to Battle Creek, where he was given a new position as vice president of trade marketing. His role was to build a bridge between the sales and marketing departments on trade promotion practices, but in practice he was more like a referee. "Salespeople were pressured by customers to do some of this stuff, and you have to say 'no,' so they're pissed because they're not making their numbers and they're blaming you for their business not being good," Straniero recalls. "At the other end, you got the marketing guys wanting to do crazy things that you know won't work, but they pressure you and they're relentless."

Straniero's expertise in trade promotions, his position as a respected mediator, and his understanding of what made Kellogg's sales force run made him one of TPE's most important champions. He was responsible for changing the name of the ROI initiative from Trade Promotion "Efficiency" to "Excellence." He wanted to appeal to the sales reps' sense of pride and felt strongly that rather than emphasizing the cool rationality of the program's efficiency, the team should stress that TPE was the next generation of sales superiority.

Straniero insisted that whatever mistakes had been made in the past were due to a lack of information, and had nothing to do with the efforts of individual sales reps' defusing the "blame game" before it began. At the same time, he made it clear to the sales force that TPE was not just the latest management whim, something that could be ignored or sabotaged. And because of his impeccable operational experience, the staff knew he was shooting straight with them.

Like many change effort champions, Straniero is demure about his role. "Selling it down wasn't hard because I had the reputation of being the trade marketing guy," he says. "The people who were running the field organization had almost all come through Battle Creek on a development project at one time or another and worked for me, so I had the bridges to get it done. And with Sue [Karibjanian] running the show, I had that support, too. At the end of the day, I think people realized it was the right, natural evolution of the business to move from art to science."

Straniero emphasizes the importance of creating champions throughout the organization. He kept division managers abreast of what was happening from the beginning, and immersed them in the program as it rolled out. He made sure that each manager had a TPE champion of his own on staff, who would help with training and solving problems. As a result of the work of all these champions at a variety of levels within Kellogg's, the focus on trade promotion excellence via ROI became a fully developed organizational capacity.

PILOTING TPE FOR A FAST START

With a compelling vision in mind and the support of its initial champions, the TPE team's next task was to begin to bring it to life. At Kellogg's, this meant that the sophisticated analytics that revealed the true nature of the company's trade promotions had to be made user-friendly in a dynamic and methodical way. If sales reps in the field were to determine which brands to promote, the nature of the promotion, and the extent of support each event should receive, they needed a set of tools that would enable them to make wise decisions, carry them out, and measure the results.

The team determined that these software-based tools had to facilitate planning; sales reps had to be able to use their laptop computers to predict the incremental volume and ROI of a specific promotion and perform simple "what-ifs" by changing one or more variables. The tools also had to link the sales reps' promotion plans into the company's financial management system (which reconciled invoices and cut checks to trade customers). And finally, the tools needed to close the learning loop via post-event analysis that would allow the sales reps and management to compare the predictions for each event with its actual results.

The TPE team streamlined the development process for these tools by forming a dedicated development team of statisticians, market researchers, and process analysts. The new team adopted an operating mindset that Doore describes as "adjust as you go" and turned the typical development process on its head. Instead of gathering user input, converting that input into program specifications, and writing code based on those specs, the implementation team quickly created mock-up screens and invited a half-dozen sales reps to critique them and help finalize the features of the tool.

In order to ensure robust results, the sales reps were chosen from a diverse set of accounts. One rep sold to wholesalers; another sold to a retailer that had "everyday low prices" that was not as responsive to trade deals; another to stores with "hi-lo" pricing policies that aggressively participated in promotions. "They were really smart about flying in sales reps from around the country to design the screens," says Phil Straniero. "They were user defined, and sequenced the way they did their work. We knew what deliverables we wanted; the sales reps told us how to get there."

With the sales reps' initial responses in hand, the implementation team produced a beta version of the planning tool within a month. Now, the reps began to use it to write real trade promotion schedules for their accounts. As you might expect, applying the tool in the real world produced plenty of tension. "There was a lot of head butting between different mindsets," recalls Kevin Reeser, one of the six salespeople. "Gearheads were trying to take the business and make it all numbers oriented, bottom line." Time and time again, the implementation team analyzed the data, made its best guesses, gathered feedback, and adjusted the model.

As the sales reps were testing the tool, the implementation team was learning important things about how they used it. For example, it quickly became apparent that if salespeople were told to focus on profit, that's precisely what they would do—to the detriment of everything else. "You can't overemphasize the return on investment, because then sales reps get competitive about who has the highest ROI, and in some cases they gave up volume that they shouldn't have given up," Straniero explains. "You've got to find a balance between meeting your revenue goal and meeting your ROI."

Once it was made clear that TPE was not just about ROI, however, the sales reps adjusted their plans, and both volume and ROI improved. Soon, the software was delivering accurate predictions, and just as important, the small core group of sales reps, who would eventually help "sell" the program to colleagues, was convinced of its efficacy.

DEMONSTRATING TPE'S SUCCESS

Pilot projects are indispensable during the development process, and their results suggest whether a marketing ROI initiative has the potential to succeed, but by nature, they are diminutive in scale. A larger demonstration is needed to create large-scale support for an initiative. In the case of TPE, that meant rolling out the new tools and process in a key market—specifically, 21 customer accounts in California.

The problem with a larger demonstration is that it involves a somewhat larger group of people—with all the additional uncertainty and resistance that entails. The Californian sales reps involved in this new test project knew that they were participating in a new program and that something big was happening, but they didn't know if TPE was for real or just a passing fad. They also wondered whether the new tools would actually help them to sell or simply inject unwelcome levels of accountability and managerial oversight into their work. The TPE team was dipping its foot into the swirling waters of cultural change.

The team established temporary planning centers in which five-day training sessions were held to dispel this uncertainty. The sessions started with an overview of TPE and its objectives, explaining how it forecasted business results and its strategic and tactical uses. The second and third days were devoted to setting up the California sales reps to succeed by helping them develop their individual plans, a process that required lots of one-on-one attention. On the fourth day, the plans were reviewed, the rules developed to guide the reps discussed, and training in how to present the plans to customers offered. The fifth day covered the implications of TPE for the sales reps' jobs, and the sessions ended with optional time for reworking plans.

The team also significantly lowered the resistance to TPE by positioning it as a reward for diligence. "We didn't hold it over their heads from a hammer point of view; we held it over their heads from an excellence point of view," says Straniero. "In other words, until you demonstrate that you're capable of doing this, we're not going to do it at your account."

Despite all the questions and problems that continued to crop up in the California test, the time and attention spent helping the sales reps to understand TPE's objectives and how it worked paid off. The majority of sales reps were able to build plans that exceeded ROI and volume targets (many generated 20 percent greater volume with no increase in spending), although considerable effort was sometimes required. In fact, by the end of the test, the primary complaint of trainees was that they could not take the new tools home with them to use immediately on their accounts.

The California test also taught the TPE team several important lessons regarding how to improve the rollout process. In later sessions, for instance, the sales reps would be provided with reading materials, including a case study, prior to the training, and more time would be allocated for hands-on account planning and teaching customer sell-in strategies.

The marked improvement in ROI and volume numbers generated in California set the stage for the companywide launch of TPE. The team was still testing and refining its newfound ROI analytics and tools, but Kellogg's top management had seen enough to send Sue Karibjanian to the boardroom to make the critical and compelling presentation for funding.

MAINTAINING TPE'S MOMENTUM AND SOLIDIFYING ITS GAINS

Kellogg's board agreed to fund the drive for profitable volume, but the money alone could not guarantee successful rollout of TPE across the company. Cultural conventions and long-established work practices, as well as departmental biases, became major obstacles. Trade customers, who had been profiting from Kellogg's promotions all along, needed to be convinced that TPE was a win-win situation. Further, the executive support that started the TPE ball rolling had to be maintained.

For a companywide implementation to succeed, the TPE team had to encourage the sales force to accept accountability for ROI, give them the tools they needed to make promotion decisions, and set them free to execute their plans. The problem was ROI represented a complete turnaround in terms of sales objectives. "Before, we weren't held accountable for anything," sales rep Reeser recalls. "As the company became more and more sophisticated, we realized that we would have to go from cost per incremental pound to a return on investment. So much of that was stuff that we, as salespeople, didn't think about. That was for headquarters to worry about."

One way that the TPE team drove accountability down the ladder was through the sharing of key "a-ha!" moments. The sales reps, like the company's executives, assumed that whatever the shortcomings of trade promotion, they were, at least, profitable for the company. But when they saw the analysis that proved that most deals were actually losing money along with the causes of these losses (for example, forward buying, wrong timing, or lack of adequate display), they began to think about planning events differently. The team further emphasized the sea change in mind-set and strategy from a volume to value sales focus by changing the reps' compensation structure. When the salespeople learned that their incentives would be tied to ROI as well as volume quotas, they naturally took TPE far more seriously.

To build momentum for a marketing ROI initiative, not only do you have to demonstrate to individuals that the company's interests are aligned with their own, you also need to deal with the entrenched biases of all of the departments that might be affected in any way. For instance, it did not take long for Kellogg's brand managers to realize that if sales was going to be responsible for determining which brands were supported at each account (as well as when they'd be promoted and for how much), they'd be losing a fair amount of control over the brands and the profit and loss.

The all-important equilibrium between sales and marketing was restored in several ways. When it became apparent that brand managers would have no control over decisions to shift funds from certain bestsellers to less visible but still important "marquee" brands because the ROI on the best sellers was far superior, the TPE team decided to allow certain deals that were not justified by the ROI alone, such as those in support of strategic brands that required more attention from the business or achieving initial distribution for new products. Further, to ensure that the sales reps, freed from the dictates of a national calendar approved by brand managers, would not offer deals that were off strategy or would undermine a brand's equity, marketing was enlisted to help develop ironclad rules—boundaries within which the sales reps had to play. There were minimum price points, for instance, as well as maximum and minimum promotion frequencies for specific brands.

A second and unexpected functional clash developed between sales and the forecasting department. The sales reps' focus on ROI created production problems as underpromoted cereals with high ROIs received more attention. For instance, Kellogg's capacity to produce "puffed" cereals was limited, and if sales volume rose too rapidly, the company might not have been able to fill orders on a timely basis. As a result, forecasting resisted TPE, afraid that with bottom-up trade planning, it would be unable to set its production schedules accurately. This situation naturally also made manufacturing anxious. The TPE team quickly created an issue resolution team to deal with these ad hoc problems. Pros and cons were presented, alternatives were discussed, and a binding decision was made on the spot. In retrospect, however, the forecasting department should have been involved in the TPE planning process far sooner than it was. "You can't involve all the ancillary departments who will be involved soon enough," says Dan Doore.

Retailers, too, were skeptical about TPE, and the sales reps had to be prepared to deal with customer resistance. Thus, the sales reps were trained to describe the customer benefits of TPE, including the new flexibility it created. For example, instead of every retailer in the market running the same deal dictated by Kellogg's headquarters—say 18-ounce boxes of Corn Flakes—at the same time, each could now differentiate itself and run specials on the products that fit their customers' wants. Now, stores could better create promotion plans that were customized to their needs in conjunction with their Kellogg's account representative.

Brad Bjorndahl, who handled the account for the huge Vons grocery store chain in Southern California, sat down with its category manager early in the process and carefully explained the tool and Kellogg's new emphasis on managing promotions for mutual ROI. Then he listened.

"If you took what the customer was trying to do and pieced it into the TPE tool, they were really excited about it," Bjorndahl says. "All of a sudden they became partners with us in trying to create a business opportunity."

The TPE team wisely recognized that in addition to maintaining the momentum of the initiative, it also had to solidify the gains it won. The team realized that just because it had enjoyed the initial support of the company's leadership, that support would not necessarily be permanent and unwavering. In response, it set up a Top Management Steering Committee that met for a half day every two to three months. This formal mechanism kept executives like Knowlton and Harris aware of the team's progress and problems, and ensured that the team had an opportunity to respond to any concerns they might have.

In order to further solidify the gains it had made, the leaders of the initiative also hired a small team with specialized skills that formed the beginnings of a center of excellence and assumed full responsibility for the analytics. The planning centers became a permanent part of the planning process, as did the institutionalization of guidelines and rules, as well as training for salespeople.

* * * *

TPE turned out to be a quite an accomplishment. Since its rollout, it has saved Kellogg's at least $65 million annually. The company's average return on marketing investment for trade promotion rose from 5 percent to between 20 percent and 25 percent. That's a lot of Sugar Pops.

TPE has also enabled Kellogg's to divert investment dollars from trade promotions to brand building and new product innovations. This helped fund a new wave of creativity and growth within the company. For instance, Special K Red Berries was so hot when it was introduced in the United States in 2001 that Kellogg's had to pull its advertising to keep up with demand. New TV ads for Kellogg's Fruit Harvest Apple Cinnamon cereal in the summer of 2003 were ranked number one for recall and likability by a panel of 135,000 consumers polled by the Intermedia Advertising Group. Kellogg's also signed a long-term licensing deal to market cereals featuring Disney characters and establish brand tie-ins with hit movies such as *Monsters, Inc.*, *Beauty and the Beast*, *Spider-Man*, and *Finding Nemo*. In 2002, the company reversed a long-standing trend and recaptured market share leadership from General Mills, a position it has maintained ever since.

The most substantial and enduring benefit of TPE, however, has been the transformation of Kellogg's sales culture: financial facts drive strategy, tactical decisions are decentralized and based on profitable growth, and compensation is tied to value creation. "For our organization, it was revolutionary," says Mike Greene, Kellogg's vice president of customer marketing. "We were really creating general managers, not just trade promotion managers. And the dialogue with our [trade] customers changed from talking about trade promotion to talking about long-term business planning—things like comarketing, supply chain, and joint advertising."

Indeed, the issues underlying the corporate embrace of marketing ROI are never just related to its first use—whether that is trade promotion, as it was at Kellogg—or any of the other aspects of marketing. The shift in long-established habits has the chance to impact all elements of the marketing mix and fuel profitable growth—in Kellogg's case helping it to profitably recapture share leadership in the cereal category.

Marketing ROI has one feature that is often lacking in other corporate changes. It is, by its nature, driven by evidence and not passion. This situation forces marketers and their peers to face the facts and reflect honestly on all that they do. The result is doing more of what works, providing a day in, day out routine that generates profitable growth one event at a time, time after time. The net result is an ever-improving organization that grows volume and profits day after day, and creates marketing professionals that can help lead their companies to sustained performance.

Epilogue

Marketing ROI renders John Wanamaker's famous lament—
"I am certain that half the money I spend in advertising is
wasted; the trouble is I do not know which half"—as obsolete
as the detachable shirt collars once sold in his department stores.
It enables marketers to enhance the connections with customers
and maximize the returns on their spending, as well as account
for their financial results with the same precision as their operational and other functional colleagues.

Marketing ROI also enables marketers to better cope with the
fundamental challenges they face in today's hypercompetitive
business environment. It helps them reach customers and establish differentiation in increasingly fragmented markets. Further,
it offers an effective means of evaluating emerging marketing
vehicles and allocating spend between disparate vehicles.

In developing their marketing ROI capabilities, marketers
capture the opportunity to contribute to the growth of their

companies, justify their claims to a central role in their companies, and expand the boundaries of their profession. Our purpose in this book has been to demystify this capability, share practical insights on how to start building it today, and most importantly, offer a methodology for approaching its development that is applicable across companies and industries.

We've described how this methodology is built on four pillars—analytics, decision support, process, and organizational alignment— and we want to reiterate that marketing ROI cannot deliver its full potential as a competitive advantage unless and until all four are in place. That means that you must have the following:

- Robust *analytics* that can separate what's working from what's not, enabling marketers to determine what is truly a big idea and what is just a clever execution
- User-friendly *decision-support systems* that allow marketers and other employees to act on the data generated by the analytics
- Redesigned business *processes* that ensure effective strategy, target setting, budgeting, tactical planning, cross-functional handoffs, and post-event analysis
- *Organizational alignment* that establishes clear decision rights within the decentralized, knowledge-based strategy. This includes training and empowering executives and staff, and developing appropriate incentives to reflect the new balance between volume and profit objectives.

The first two pillars are the toolset of marketing ROI. With sophisticated software, you can direct your marketing investments to the offers, events, pricing, product adaptations, vehicles, and territories that will generate profitable growth. But the tools, and the science behind them, as exotic as they are, are only the starting point.

Marketing ROI is not just a set of tools; it is also a capability. The latter two pillars contain the elements that ensure that the toolset is fully integrated and properly utilized. To successfully develop this capability, an organization must undertake transformative change across and, often, beyond the company simultaneously, dealing with the resulting pain and upheaval. Overcoming the organizational resistance this often creates requires winning the hearts and minds of employees throughout the broader organization.

Finally, although creating a marketing ROI capability will be hard and, sometimes, daunting work, it is worth the effort. Pick a place to start, get going, and don't stop. If you do this work properly, soon you will have a marketing organization that is continuously improving its creative output, that is fully accountable for its spending and activities, and that can improve profitability by making better, faster resource allocation decisions across products, offers, markets, and vehicles. As a result, you will outperform your competitors. Tomorrow's rewards—the largest share of your customers' wallets and the most attractive profit margins—will go to the marketing leaders and the companies that begin building a sustainable capability for profit-driven marketing today.

Endnotes

INTRODUCTION

1. Unless otherwise noted, the statistics, surveys, examples, and quotes used throughout the book were developed and gathered by the authors, Booz & Company, and strategy + business.

2. "ANA Marketing Accountability Task Force Findings." *ANA*, October 8, 2005: p. 3.

3. "Marketing Outlook 2007." CMO Council, 2007: p. 2.

4. Philip Kotler, "Why CEOS Are Fed Up with Marketing." *Strategy*, May 3, 2004: p. 14.

5. "Define & Align the CMO." CMO Council, 2007: p. 12.

6. John Quelch and Gail J. McGovern, "Boards Must Measure Marketing Effectiveness." *Directors & Boards*, Spring 2006: p. 53.

7. Thomas H. Davenport, Don Cohen, and Al Jacobsen, "Competing on Analytics." Babson Executive Education Working Knowledge Research Report, May 2005; Thomas H. Davenport and Jeanne G. Harris, *Competing on Analytics.* Harvard Business School Press, 2007: p. 25.

CHAPTER 1

1. www.technorati.com/about, June 3, 2008.

2. Alvin Toffler, *The Third Wave*. William Morrow and Company, 1980: p. 153.

3. "Competitive Media Facts: Broadcast TV." Radio Advertising Bureau (http://www.rab.com/station/mediafact/mftv.html); "NBC Has One of Worst Week's Ever." The Associated Press, April 18, 2007 (http://www.cnn.com/2007/SHOWBIZ/TV/04/18/nielsens.ap/index.html).

4. "Daily Newspaper Readership Trend—Total Adults (1964–1997)" and "Daily Newspaper Readership Trend—Total Adults (1998–2006)." Newspaper Association of America (http://www.naa.org/Trends-and-Numbers/Consumer-Research/Readership-Statistics.aspx); Scarborough Research, "Top 50 Market Report 1998–2007."

5. "Radio Listening Trends: FA93-FA06 Weekly Cume/TSL." Aribitron, Inc., 2007.

6. Kaiser Family Foundation, Simultaneous Media Usage Survey by Big Research.

7. Booz & Company analysis based on data from Veronis Suhler, PQ Media, Adams Media Research, Alexander & Associates, Arbitron, and Ball State University Media Design Center.

8. "EricssonTargets More Business in China and India." *Global Insight*, June 15, 2007: p. 34.

9. Regis McKenna, "Marketing Is Everything." *Harvard Business Review*, January–February 1991: pp. 65–79.

10. Diane Brady, "The Immelt Revolution." *BusinessWeek*, March 28, 2005: p. 29.

11. Market-to-book multiples calculated by Standard & Poor's, a division of The McGraw-Hill Companies, Inc.

12. "Total GDP, 2005." World Development Indicators database, World Bank, April 23, 2007.

13. "ANA Marketing Accountability Task Force Findings." *ANA*, October 8, 2005: p. 3.

14. Greg Welch, "CMO Tenure: Slowing Down the Revolving Door." Spencer Stuart, July 2004; p. 1; "Turnover of Chief Marketing Officers Continues to Increase." Spencer Stuart, August 14, 2006; "Chief Marketing Officer Tenure Improves According to Annual Spencer Stuart Study." Spencer Stuart, June 1, 2007.

15. "CEO Challenge 2006: Perspectives & Analysis." The Conference Board, p. 6.

16. "Define & Align the CMO." CMO Council, 2007: p. 4.

17. "Most Financial Executives Critical of Marketing Effectiveness Measures." *Marketing Management Analytics*, March 13, 2007.

CHAPTER 2

1. Peter F. Drucker, *Management*. Harper & Row, 1974: pp. 61–63.

2. John F. Love, *McDonald's: Behind the Arches*. Bantam Books, 1986: pp. 207, 303–322; Sumita Vaid Dixit, "On Record." Dainik Jagran, March 7, 2005 (www.agencyfaqs.com/news/interviews/data/248.html); "The Burger That Conquered the Country." *Time*, September 17, 1973: pp. 84–92; "Top 100 Advertising Campaigns." *Advertising Age*, 1999 (http://adage.com/century/campaigns.html).

3. James R. Stengel, "Ultimate Marketers" in Geoffrey Precourt, ed., *CMO Thought Leaders: The Rise of the Strategic Marketer*. strategy + business Books, 2007 (www.strategy-business.com).

4. Phil Dusenberry, *Then We Set His Hair On Fire*. Portfolio, 2005: pp. 3–4.

5. Phil Rosenzweig, *The Halo Effect ... and the Eight Other Business Delusions That Deceive Managers*. Free Press, 2007: pp. 64, 98–99.

CHAPTER 3

1. Christopher H. Paige, "Capital One Financial Corporation." *Harvard Business School,* May 1, 2001: case 9-700-124; p. 4.

2. Miriam Leuchter, "Capital One: Fanaticism That Works." *US Banker*, August 2001: p. 75.

3. Jennifer Kingson Bloom, "Capital One Says It's Riding a Tech Revolution." *American Banker*, September 9, 1998: p. 75.

4. Paige, p. 6.

5. Leuchter.

6. Bloom.

CHAPTER 4

1. "Rob Malcolm: Spirits and Growth" in Geoffrey Precourt, ed., *CMO Thought Leaders: The Rise of the Strategic Marketer.* strategy + business Books, 2007: p. 233.

2. "Jerri DeVard: Trust and Adaptablity" in Geoffrey Precourt, ed., *CMO Thought Leaders: The Rise of the Strategic Marketer.* strategy + business Books, 2007: p 73.

3. "ANA/Booz & Company Study of Marketing Organizations." First phase, June–September 2004.

4. "ANA Marketing Accountability Task Force Findings." *ANA*, October 8, 2005: p. 5.

5. Catherine Arnst, "IMS Health: Where The Best Medicine Is Data." *BusinessWeek*, June 25, 2007 (http://www.business-week.com/magazine/content/07_26/b4040057.htm).

6. The ACNielsen Company case is based on author interviews with current and former employees, including Mitchell Kriss, John Porter, Marshall White, and Dick Wittink.

7. "Marketing Mix Modeling Moves into the Boardroom." DemandGen Report (http://www.demandgenreport.com/archive.php?codearti=1003).

8. "BrandAsset Valuator: BAV 101." Young &Rubicam presentation, February 2007.

CHAPTER 5

1. Meridith Levinson, "Harrah's Knows What You Did Last Night." *CIO*, June 6, 2001.

2. Del Jones, "Client Data Means Little Without Good Analysis." *USA Today*, December 24, 2001: http://www.usatoday.com/money/general/2001/12/24/crm.htm.

3. The Harrah's example is based on author interviews with CEO and chairman Gary Loveman and Richard Mirman, formerly senior vice president of new business development.

4. Paul Sloan, "The Quest for the Perfect Online Ad." *Business 2.0*, March 2007: http://money.cnn.com/magazines/business2/business2_archive/2007/03/01/8401043/index.htm.

5. "ANA Marketing Accountability Task Force Findings." *ANA*, October 8, 2005: p. 16.

CHAPTER 6

1. "Procter & Gamble: The Importance of Attitude," in Rob Norton, ed., *CFO Thought Leaders: Advancing the Frontiers of Finance.* strategy + business Books, 2005: pp. 90–91.

2. Ibid.

3. Yoji Akao, ed., *Hoshin Kanri: Policy Deployment for Successful TQM.* Productivity Press, 1991.

4. "Olaf Göttgens: Premium Product Development," in Geoffrey Precourt, ed., *CMO Thought Leaders: The Rise of the Strategic Marketer*, strategy + business Books, 2007: pp. 167–168.

CHAPTER 7

1. "ANA Marketing Accountability Task Force Findings." *ANA*, October 8, 2005: p. 9.

2. Ibid.

CHAPTER 8

1. The Kellogg's Trade Promotion Excellence case is based on Booz & Company's engagement with the company and interviews with current and former Kellogg's managers and executives, including Scott Barnes, Brad Bjorndahl, Jim Burt, Dan Doore, Bob Dow, Pete Galster, Mike Greene, Carolyn Gawlinski Hendricksma, Sue Karibjanian, Tom Knowlton, Dale Lazarro, Amjad Malik, Kevin Reeser, Phil Straniero, and Adonis Vergara.

2. Jeffrey G. Kanter, "Kellogg Company—A Global Icon." Salomon Brothers, October 10, 1997: pp. 18–19.

Index

About the Authors

Leslie H. Moeller (leslie.moeller@booz.com) is a partner at Booz & Company. Based in the Cleveland office, he is the Consumer & Media Practice Leader for North America. Les works to enhance the ability of major companies to generate revenue through marketing and pricing effectiveness, improved channel management, and proven growth and innovation strategies.

In his 16 years with Booz & Company, Les has helped successfully implement marketing ROI strategies and systems at consumer product companies that sell everything from soup to nuts, as well as tires, mouthwash, washing machines, cell phones, windows, and fertilizer. Les is a two-time recipient of the Professional Excellence Award, the highest professional distinction awarded by Booz & Company. He began his career and learned the marketing profession in a six-year stint in brand management at Procter & Gamble, where he worked on a variety of brands, including NyQuil, Formula 44, Fixodent, Folgers, Citrus Hill, and Pampers.

Les is the lead author of "The Better Half: The Artful Science of ROI Marketing," which appeared in *strategy + business* magazine and served as the impetus for this book. He has also written and contributed to many other $s + b$ articles, including "The Superpremium Premium," "10x Growth: The Engine Powering Long-Term Shareholder Returns," "Smart Customization: Profitable Growth through Tailored Business Streams," and "A Clear Look at Biofuels."

A cum laude graduate of Harvard College with an A.B. in philosophy, Les lives with his wife and three children on Hensbury Farm in Waite Hill, Ohio.

Edward C. Landry (edward.landry@booz.com) is a partner at Booz & Company. Based in the firm's New York office, he is a member of the Consumer & Media practice. He focuses on strategy development, business transformation, and sales and marketing effectiveness across a broad range of consumer businesses.

Ed has two decades of experience in consumer products industries including food, beverage, household, personal care, and healthcare companies. Since joining Booz & Company in 1996, he has worked with the senior management of many leading global companies to develop innovative growth strategies, strengthen operating performance, and redesign organization structures. Ed is also a recipient of Booz & Company's Professional Excellence Award. Prior to joining the firm, he held positions in marketing, strategic planning, and international business development at Procter & Gamble and RJR Nabisco.

Ed leads Booz & Company's ongoing research on marketing organization effectiveness and accountability with the Association of National Advertisers, and has written extensively about marketing and sales strategy and effectiveness. He coauthored the book *CMO Thought Leaders: The Rise of the Strategic Marketer* (strategy + business Books, 2007). He has also written and collaborated on numerous articles appearing in *Advertising Age*, *strategy + business*, and other publications, including "Success Means Slimming Down Brand Portfolios," "Growth Champions: How to Drive the Only Marketing Metric That Matters," "Making the Perfect Marketer," "Engineering Your Organization's DNA For Growth," and "The Adaptive Sales Force."

Ed holds an MBA from the Kenan-Flagler Business School at the University of North Carolina at Chapel Hill, where he served as teaching assistant for Crist W. Blackwell Distinguished Professor of Marketing Gary Armstrong, and a B.A. in economics with a minor in government and law from Lafayette College. He lives with his wife and four children in Vienna, Virginia, a suburb of Washington D.C.

Theodore Kinni (tedkinni@cox.net) is senior editor of strategy + business Books, overseeing the creation of Booz & Company Readers and assisting in the editing of the McGraw-Hill/strategy + business series, *The Future of Business*. He has authored and collaborated on 12 other business books, including *Be Our Guest: Perfecting the Art of Customer Service* for the Walt Disney Company and *America's Best: IndustryWeek's Guide to World-Class Manufacturing Plants*.

Ted is an active freelance business writer whose articles and book reviews have appeared in many periodicals, including *Business 2.0, Chief Executive, Consulting, Harvard Management Update, Conference Board Review, Training*, and *Selling Power*. He has also served as contributing editor for *IndustryWeek, Quality Digest*, and *Workforce Training News*.

Ted is a member of the National Book Critics Circle and the Society of American Business Editors and Writers. He lives in Williamsburg, Virginia, with his spouse and writing partner, Donna.